Spanish in a week
Master the basics of Spanish in 7 days

By Lucy Martin

With thanks to my proof readers Anthony Morris and Louise Lacourarie

And to the Spanish, for making things relatively simple for English speaking beginners….

Copyright Lucy Martin 2018

Table of contents

Introduction												5

Day 1												13
Gender, articles, verbs and adjectives, the present tense

Day 2												23
Infinitives and their uses – the future tense

Day 3												33
The past tense

Day 4												41
Ser, estar, tener and *hay*

Day 5												53
Pronouns and liking

Day 6												61
Reflexive verbs and the verb *hacer*

Day 7												69
The personal *a*

Verb tables and vocabulary										81

Introduction

Spanish in a week? Yes you can! I believe that anyone who wants to get to grips with the basics of the language can do so in these seven lessons.

What will I learn?
Obviously not everything there is to know. Not even a fraction of it. But you will be able to express yourself, your likes, dislikes and problems, ask and answer basic questions, talk about your life, your family, the things you have done and plan to do. Most importantly, you will learn about the structure of the language, which will pave the way for more study, if you choose to take it further.

How long should I spend?
Some will race through them, others will take longer to complete the daily chapters, but I have in mind about an hour a day. If this is not enough time, take two days per chapter. Don't rush. There are no prizes except the satisfaction of having made progress. If you find you cover it faster than you thought, repeat the exercises to consolidate and look at the vocabulary lists at the end of the book. I can also highly recommend a website **www.notesinspanish.com** and **www.videoele.com** which does superb videos for Spanish learners of all levels. You can also try **www.newsinslowspanish.com** where you can listen and read along with current news stories, hovering over difficult words to see their meaning.

What if I need support?
Language is all about speaking and listening, and here I am teaching you through writing and reading. Clearly you need an extra dimension to complete the picture. Firstly, I am here to answer your questions. Just get in touch via my website **www.lucymartintuition.co.uk**. Secondly, make use of the videoele website above. Thirdly, I am in the process of developing some online materials that will link to my website when complete.

I wish you all the best with your exciting week of Spanish, and I welcome your feedback through my website www.lucymartintuition.co.uk.

Telling you what you already know....

The great news is that you already know a lot of Spanish. Like most Latin-based languages, it is full of words that you can guess quite easily. These are called cognates. There are "perfect" cognates which are the same as the English, and there are those which differ slightly but are guessable.

Words ending in -al in English tend to be the same in Spanish

animal, artificial, brutal, capital, central, criminal, formal, final, general, global, horizontal, hospital, ideal, informal, industrial, legal, local, material, mental, metal, musical, natural, normal, oral, original, personal, regional, sentimental, social, rural, social, universal, verbal, vertical

Other perfect cognates

drama, hotel, horror, terror, invisible, inferior, superior, inevitable, control, idea, error, cancer, cheque, chocolate, club, flexible

Words in -tion in English are -ción in Spanish and they are all feminine

reservación, conversación, contaminación, acción, atención, colaboración, clasificación, colección, combinación, concentración, condición, construcción, nación, operación, discriminación, publicación

Words in -ty in English are -dad and they are all feminine

universidad, sociedad, ciudad (city), calidad (quality), capacidad, comunidad, curiosidad, deformidad, dificultad, cantidad (quantity), velocidad, diversidad, creatividad, celebridad

Words ending in -ic or -ical in English are usually -ico in Spanish

académico, artístico, económico, automático, básico, democrático, clásico, exótico, fantástico, heroico, irónico, mágico, orgánico, plástico, público, romántico, político, psicológico, biológico, físico, cómico

You can also add an o to words ending in ct in English

adicto, conflicto, contacto, correcto, exacto, insecto, perfecto, producto

English words ending in -ous tend to end in -oso in Spanish

religioso, curioso, delicioso, misterioso, tedioso, numeroso, varioso

Not like English but familiar to the English!

Hola amigo	hello friend
Buenos días	hello, good morning
Gracias	thank you
Por favor	please
Señor, Señora, Señorita	sir, madam, miss

Food and drink

dos cervezas	two beers
sangría	sangria
vino	wine
paella	spanish rice dish
ortilla	spanish omelette
chorizo	spicy sausage
tapas	bar snacks

From your knowledge of geography

Costa Blanca	literally – white coast
Costa del Sol	literally – coast of the sun
Costa Brava	literally – wild coast
Costa Rica	literally – rich coast
Puerto Rico	literally – rich port

Phrases from songs

Que será será	what will be will be
Vamos a la playa	we go (let's go) to the beach
Viva España	long live Spain
Hasta mañana	until tomorrow
despacito	slowly

From the movies

los pollos hermanos	the *"chicken brothers"* (Breaking Bad)
Hasta la vista	*see you later* – from Terminator 2
Qué?	*What?* – Manuel from Fawlty Towers
Mi casa, su casa	My house, your house

SO what do these mean?

Un animal brutal

Un error universal

Un club local

Un criminal psicológico

Pizza deliciosa

Una publicación legal

Un problema global

Un hospital básico

Un adicto clásico

Una condición universal

Una idea central

Un producto orgánico

Una capacidad superior

Una sociedad democrática

Una calidad inferior

Una nación perfecta

Una reacción automática

Places in town that you'll recognise

el parque	park
el colegio	school
el supermercado	supermarket
el mercado	market
el centro comercial	shopping centre
el hotel	hotel
el teatro	theatre
el cine	cinema

Words that make sense when you take off the e at the front

estómago	stomach
espinacas	spinach
estudiantes	students
estación	station
estable	stable
estadio	stadium
escándalo	scandal
escenario	scandal
Escocia	Scotland
escuela	school
espacio	space
España	Spain
especial	special
espectador	spectator
espinal	spinal
esposo	spouse / husband
esposa	spouse / wife
esquí	skiing
estatua	statue
estrés	stress
estricto	strict
estupendo	amazing (stupendous)

Words that have cognates in French

Don't worry if you don't speak French, but if you do, here is a list of words that you will recognise:

biblioteca	library
fácil	easy
difícil	difficult
malo	bad
mal	badly
bicicleta	bike
jardí	garden
grande	big
enorme	enormous
tranquilo	quiet
simpático	nice
avión	plane
pan	bread
té	tea
fresas	strawberries
frambuesas	raspberries
viejo	old
bien	well
aprender	to learn
el mar	sea
fumar	to smoke
profesor	teacher

There are plenty of other words in Spanish that you will know the meaning of when you hear them.

Read this for example. You'll understand it and you haven't even begun day 1

Londres es la capital de Inglaterra y en Londres hay muchos sitios turísticos maravillosos. Hay palacios, galerías, estatuas estupendas, museos y restaurantes, teatros, conciertos de música clásica y moderna, cines, cafés, parques, y hoteles lujosos. Mis sitios favoritos son el museo de las ciencias y el zoo, donde hay animales exóticos de todas partes del planeta, incluso elefantes, serpientes y pingüinos. Los turistas visitan Londres para admirar la arquitectura y estudiar la cultura inglesa. La historia de Inglaterra es extremadamente interesante. El único problema en Londres es el tráfico que causa la contaminación del aire, y es un problema no solo regional. Es un problema global. Necesitamos soluciones para resolver los problemas. La primera solución es usar el transporte publico. En Londres los autobuses rojos son famosos y las bicicletas municipales son fenomenales.

London is the capital of England and in London there are many marvellous tourist sights. There are palaces, galleries, amazing statues, museums and restaurants, theatres, classical and modern music concerts and luxurious hotels are luxurious. My favourite places are the science museum and the zoo, where there are exotic animals from all over the world including elephants, snakes and penguins. Tourists visit London to admire the architecture and study English culture. The history of England is extremely interesting. The only problem in London is the traffic which causes air pollution, and it is is not just a local problem. It is a global problem. The first solution is to use the public transport and in London the red buses are famous and the municipal bicycles are fantastic.

Sounds and spellings

Spanish is very phonetic, so great if you have any dyslexic tendencies, and one of the easiest languages to learn from a book.

Que – sounds like the letter K in English (porque – *"poor Kay"* – because, quiero – "key aero" – I want)

Ll - double ll is pronounced as a y (llegar – *"yeggar"* – to arrive)

J – always a guttural h as if you are clearing your throat

G – guttural like j above, when before i or e, otherwise a g as in *go*

H – silent as it is in French (helado – *"elado"* – ice cream)

Z – "th" (empezar – *"empethar"* – to begin)

C – "th" before i and e, otherwise a normal c

S – soft as in "sofa", never hard as in "realise"

R – always rolled, as if you are freezing cold and saying "Brrrrrrrr"

Ñ – the wiggly line turns it into "ny" as in España and mañana

Vowels are phonetic – *a* as in *cat*, *e* as in *get*, *i* like the *ee* in *he*, *o* as in *dog* and *u* as in the vowel sound in *do*

Accents – There is only one type of accent and it exists mainly to mark stress on the syllable, where the stress wouldn't necessarily naturally fall there eg. lápiz, escándalo, dificil.

Double letters are rare – except perro (dog) or aburrido (boring)

Questions are surrounded by question marks ¿Cuantos años tienes?

Same goes with exclamations   ¡Que desastre!

Day 1 – gender, articles, verbs and adjectives

Gender of nouns

Spanish nouns are masculine or feminine. Mostly you can tell a feminine noun because it ends in an -*a*.

BUT there are a few nouns ending in -*ma* that are masculine *(el problema, el programa),* and others in -*a* eg. *el día, el mapa, el sofá, el planeta.*

Conversely, nouns ending in -*dad* are feminine, and correspond to English words ending in -*ity* eg. l*a universidad, la sociedad, la posibilidad.*

All nouns ending in *ation* in English end in *ación* in Spanish and they are all feminine eg. *la reservación, la conversación.*

Articles

There are 4 words for "the" in Spanish depending on whether the noun is masculine or feminine and singular or plural:

el perro	the dog
la chica	the girl
los chicos	the boys
las casas	the houses

There are two words for "a" depending on whether the noun is masculine or feminine:

un gato	a cat
un día	a day
una mesa	a table
una reservación	a reservation

Add an "s" or "os" for "some"

unos coches	some cars
unas cervezas	some beers

Verbs in the present tense

Conjugating a verb means adapting it to the person who is doing it. In English, present tense conjugation is mostly straightforward. We keep the verb the same whoever is doing it, except that with the he/she/it form we add an s *(I eat, you eat, he/she eats, we eat, you eat, they eat)*.

We need to conjugate verbs in Spanish, but we don't need to include the pronoun. The ending of the verb tells you who is doing it. So, for example, if you see a *"mos"* on the end of a verb, the person who is doing it is going to be "we". *"Visitamos"* means *"we visit"*.

Although you don't have to use the pronouns (I, you, he, she, it, we, they), it is sometimes useful to know them for the purposes of your understanding, and for clarity or emphasis:

yo	I
tú	you (singular)
él	he
ella	she
usted	you (singular polite form)
nosotros	we
vosotros	you (plural)
ellos	they (masculine or mixed group)
ellas	they (feminine group)
ustedes	you (plural polite form)

You will notice a few things about this list. Firstly, there are two words for *"they"* depending on whether the group referred to is exclusively feminine or not. So, if you are talking about houses (casas), it would be *"ellas"*, otherwise *"ellos"*.

Secondly, they have the polite "you" form that we don't have in English. In this book I am only using the familiar "tu" form, but the polite form is conjugated exactly like the *el / ella* form, or the *ellos / ellas* form depending on whether it is singular or plural.

Type 1 verbs ending in -*ar*

Hablar   to speak

Hablo   I speak
Hablas   you (singular) speak
Habla   he, she or it speaks
Hablamos   we speak
Habláis   you (plural) speak
Hablan   they speak

Type 2 verbs ending in -er

Comer   to eat

Como   I eat
Comes   you (singular) eat
Come   he, she or it eats
Comemos   we eat
Coméis   you (plural) eat
Comen   they eat

Type 3 verbs ending in -ir

Vivir   to live

Vivo   I live
Vives   you (singular) live
Vive   he, she or it lives
Vivimos   we live
Vivís   you (plural) live
Viven   they live

A pattern begins to emerge. The I form ends in an o, the he form ends in a/e, the we form ends in *mos* and the they form always ends in an n.

Practise with these

hablan	they speak
viven	they live
vive	he/she lives
come	he/she eats
comemos	we eat
hablamos	we speak
hablo	I speak
vivo	I live
vivimos	we live
fuman	they smoke
habla	he/she speaks
visito	I visit
aprendo	I learn
fumamos	we smoke
aprenden	they learn
reciclamos	we recycle
habláis	you (pl) speak
visitamos	we visit
estudian	they study
visitan	they visit
comen	they eat
reciclo	I recycle
estudio	I study
aprendemos	we learn
fumo	I smoke
reciclan	they recycle
como	I eat
reservan	they reserve
comunicamos	we communicate
causa	it causes
uso	I use
preparas	you prepare
reservamos	we reserve
vivimos	we live
usan	they use
estudias	you study
visitáis	you (pl) visit

Adjectives

Adjectives usually go after the noun and will agree with it in gender and number. This means that if it ends in an *o*, this changes to an *a* if the noun it describes is feminine. If it ends in *-or* this changes to *-ora,* and they all get an extra *s* on the end (*-es* in the case of the ones ending in *-or*) if the noun they describe is plural. Adjectives ending in *e* like *inteligente* can't change to *a*, so they only agree in number.

Un perro grande, blanco y español – a big white Spanish dog

Unos perros grandes, blancos y españoles – big white Spanish dogs

Una casa grande, blanca, y española – a big white Spanish house

Unas casas grandes, blancas y españolas – big white Spanish houses

Practise these a few times - learning some new vocabulary (en, son, con) as well as putting together the work so far.

Vivimos en casas interesantes	We live in interesting houses
Comen tapas españolas	They eat Spanish tapas
Reciclo muchas botellas	I recycle a lot of bottles
Vivo en un apartamento grande	I live in a big apartment
El colegio es enorme	The school is enormous
Las pizzas son deliciosas	(The) pizzas are delicious
Hablo con personas inteligentes	I talk to clever people

Possessive adjectives

Possessive adjectives go in front of and agree just in number with the noun they refer to. So, the word for *my* when we say *my sister* (mi hermana) is different from when we say *my brothers* (mis hermanos). Here they all are:

mi hermano / hermana	my brother / sister
mis padres	my parents
tus hermanos / hermanas	your brothers / sisters
tus padres	your parents
su hermano / hermana	his, her or their brother / sister
sus padres	his, her or their parents
nuestro(s) hermano(s)	our brother(s)
nuestra(s) hermana(s)	our sister(s)
vuestro(s) hermano(s)	your (from you *pl*) brother(s)
vuestra(s) hermana(s)	your (from you *pl*) sister(s)

Some new vocabulary for the test below

(no) tengo	I have / don't have
(no) hay (pronounced "I")	there is/isn't
(no) soy	I am / I'm not

Test on the basics – repeat until you can put all the sentences into Spanish. Concentrate on getting the article (a/the) right and making the verb agree with the subject, and adjectives agree with nouns.

1.	They live in the house	Viven en la casa
2.	We live in a big house	Vivimos en una casa grande
3.	They live in his house	Viven en su casa
4.	The girls eat their fruit	Las chicas comen su fruta
5.	He lives in his apartment	Vive en su apartamento
6.	We eat lots of pizza	Comemos mucha pizza
7.	I have two big cars	Tengo dos coches grandes
8.	I don't have sisters	No tengo hermanas
9.	He speaks to my parents	Habla con mis padres
10.	We are speaking to my teacher	Hablamos con mi profesor
11.	There are some dogs in the park	Hay unos perros en el parque
12.	We don't speak Spanish	No hablamos español
13.	They don't speak English	No hablan inglés
14.	My parents live in Spain	Mis padres viven en España
15.	My children live in London	Mis amigos viven en Londres
16.	His brother doesn't eat pasta	Su amigo no come pasta
17.	There are good beaches in Spain	Hay playas buenas en España
18.	The teachers are good	Los profesores son buenos
19.	My parents are strict	Mis padres son estrictos
20.	There are two beers here	Hay dos cervezas aquí

Dialogue 1

Pilar y Juan Carlos, dos personas solitarias están en un bar en Barcelona.

P: ¿Hola, soy Pilar, y tú?

JC: Soy Juan Carlos

P: Encantada

JC: ¿Dónde vives?

P: Vivo en una casa enorme en la playa con diez dormitorios y un cine. Hay una piscina en el jardín. Soy muy rica. Tengo dos hijos. Rafael vive en Madrid con su familia y Pedro vive en mi casa.

JC: ¿Rica? ¿Piscina? ¿Cine? No tengo casa, y necesito un cine y una piscina. La playa es mi sitio favorito porque no hay tráfico.

P: Soy creativa, flexible, artística, interesante, inteligente y vulnerable. Tengo dos coches grandes y no tengo animales.

JC: Perfecto.

P: ¿Y tú?

JC: Yo también soy interesante, flexible, estable, y muy muy romántico.

P: ¡Estupendo! Vamos a mi casa imediatamente.

Translation of dialogue 1

Pilar and Juan Carlos, two lonely people, are in a bar in Barcelona.

P: Hello, I am Pilar, and you?

JC: I am Juan Carlos.

P: Delighted to meet you.

JC: Where do you live?

P: I live in an enormous house on the beach with ten bedrooms and a cinema. There is a swimming pool in the garden. I am very rich. I have two children. Rafael lives in Madrid with his family and Pedro lives in my house.

JC: Rich? Pool? Cinema? I don't have a house and I need a cinema and a pool. The beach is my favourite place because there is no traffic.

P: I am creative, flexible, artistic, interesting, intelligent and vulnerable. I have two big cars and I don't have any pets.

JC: Perfect.

P: And you?

JC: I am also interesting, flexible, stable, and very, very romantic.

P: Fantastic! Let's go to my house immediately.

Recap Day 1

- Spanish is easy to understand. We have seen the huge number of cognates in the lists before the first chapter.

- Spanish nouns are masculine and feminine, and adjectives, usually placed after the noun, must agree with the noun.

- Possessive adjectives agree with the noun, not the person that owns it.

- Verbs tell a story by themselves. We don't need to say who did it because the ending does that for us.

- The main endings for the present that we need to remember are o, a/e, mos and n.

- Pilar needs to be more careful when picking up men in bars.

- Revision of new vocabulary

soy	I am
tengo	I have
hay	there is
hablan	they speak
viven	they live
vive	he/she lives
come	he/she eats
comemos	we eat
hablamos	we speak
hablo	I speak
vivo	I live
vivimos	we live

NOTES

Day 2 – infinitives and the future tense

Take a look at this list of INFINITIVES with memory techniques

hablar	to speak (think blah blah)
ayudar	to help (take out the u and get ayd – aid_
llegar	to arrive (on your legs)
salir	to go out (with Sally)
volver	to return (revolving doors)
comer	to eat (come 'ere to eat)
tocar	to touch or play (toc toc toc)
sacar	to take (out of the sack)
bailar	to dance (ballet)
limpiar	to clean (imagine limping afterwards)
trabajar	to work (go to a lot of trouble)
vender	to sell (vending machine)
ver	to watch (a very good programme)
beber	to drink (baby drinks milk)
viajar	to travel (voyage)
recibir	to receive (b = v)
esperar	to wait for / hope (going spare!)
buscar	to look for (a bus or a car)
pensar en	to think about (tapping a pen on your head thinking)
olvidar	to forget (forget about Olly)
comprender	to understand (comprehend)
aprender	to learn (apprentice)
compartir	to share (divide into compartments)
fumar	to smoke (fumes)

No techniques for these yet!

tener (que)	to have (to)
ser	to be
ir	to go
hacer	to do (pronounced "athair"
vivir	to live
comprar	to sell
escuchar	to listen to
jugar	to play

Brilliant uses of infinitives

1. **To say what you like and don't like – me gusta**

No me gusta trabajar	I don't like working
Me gusta dormir	I like sleeping

2. **To say what you usually do - suelo**

Suelo comer mucha fruta	I usually eat a lot of fruit
No suelo llegar tarde	I don't usually arrive late
Suelo beber té	I usually drink tea
No suelo limpiar la casa	I don't usually clean the house

3. **To say what you have to or can do – tengo que**

Tengo que salir	I have to go out
Tenemos que trabajar	We have to work
No tengo que ir	I don't have to go
No tenemos que escuchar	We don't have to listen

4. **To say what you can do – puedo**

¿Puedo venir?	Can I come?
¿Pueden salir?	Can they go out?
No puedo hacer mucho	I can't do much

5. **To say what you want to do – quiero**

Quiero comprar un bocadillo	I want to buy a sándwich
Quieren ir al cine	They want to go to the cinema

6. **To make the FUTURE TENSE – voy a**

Voy a vivir en España	I am going to live in Spain
No voy a comer mucho	I am not going to eat much

Read the Spanish and test yourself

I am going to clean the car	Voy a limpiar el coche
I am not going to share my house	No voy a compartir mi casa
I want to play the piano	Quiero tocar el piano
I usually understand	Suelo comprender
I don't usually live in France	No suelo vivir en Francia
I like learning Spanish	Me gusta aprender el español
I don't like dancing	No me gusta bailar
I can't go out	No puedo salir
I have to work	Tengo que trabajar
I have to speak Spanish	Tengo que hablar español

Make up a paragraph about yourself, saying what you like and don't like doing, what you have to do, what you usually do, and something about your future plans (en el futuro).

Using the future tense with other people

But what if someone else is going to do it? We need to change our "voy" to suit the person – we need to conjugate the verb "ir". Otherwise we are saying "you *am* going to do it". Here is how the verb goes: (remember we don't need the person, because the ending tells us who the person is who is doing the action).

ir = to go
voy	I go (or am going)
vas	you go
va	he / she / it goes
vamos	we go
vais	you (plural) go
van	they go

Examples of this future tense in action – don't forget the a

No vamos a salir	We are not going to go out
Van a trabajar	They are going to work
Vamos a comer tapas	We are going to eat tapas
Voy a visitar sitios turísticos	I'm going to visit tourist sights
Van a ir a la playa	They are going to go to the beach
Voy a dormir	I am going to sleep
¿Vas a jugar?	Are you going to play?
¿Vais a ir?	Are you (pl) going to go?
Va a vivir en España	He / she is going to live in Spain
¿No vas a venir?	Aren't you going to come?
No voy a comprender	I am not going to understand
No va a jugar	He / she is not going to play
No voy a beber	I'm not going to drink
Vamos a ver…	We shall see…
Vas a olvidar	You are going to forget
No voy a olvidar	I am not going to forget
Vamos a hablar español	We are going to learn Spanish
Van a tocar el piano	They are going to play the piano
Vas a compartir el vino	You are going to share the wine
No va a beber cerveza	S/he isn't going to drink beer
Voy a llegar tarde	I'm going to arrive late
No van a llegar	They aren't going to arrive

Adding to infinitives

Jugar al futbol / tenis / golf – to play football
Rule of thumb is that when you play something – use *al* before the sport or game, and they are mostly the same word as English (cricket, hockey, rugby) but with a more phonetic spelling – *voleibol, tenis, netbol*.

Hacer deporte – to do sport
We don't "play" sport, we do it. It's the same with all the non-ball sports, you *hacer* most of them – *jogging, ciclismo, vela, patinaje* (jogging, cycling, sailing, skating).

Ver la tele – to watch TV
Remember to say *la* tele because in English we just "watch TV".

Ir al trabajo / al colegio en coche – to go to work / school by car
Al, which literally means "to the" is a condensation of *a* and *el*. Sometimes it's logical (*"al* cine" means *"to the* cinema") but we have to remember that we go "to *the* work", not just to work. Same for "colegio" below.

Ir al trabajo / al colegio a pie – to go to work / school on foot
We had "by car" above, but if you are not taking any transport, "a".

Ir de compras – to go shopping

Preparar la comida / cena – to cook lunch / dinner
They tend to prepare rather than make or cook food.

Hablar con mis amigos – to talk to my friends
You talk with people, not to them.

Escuchar música - to listen to music (the "to" is built in)

Time to talk about the future...

Below, work out what the underlined words mean before looking at the translation. First, look at how we use the verb *tener – to have*.
Tengo – I have
Tienes – you have
Tiene – s/he has
Tenemos / we have
Tenéis – you (pl) have
Tienen – they have

El próximo fin de semana, voy a ir al trabajo en coche. <u>Soy</u> profesora de español y suelo trabajar <u>por la mañana</u> <u>durante</u> el fin de semana. ¡Qué pena! Voy a trabajar durante tres horas y luego voy a ir de compras y voy a volver a casa para preparar la comida para mis hijos, Juan y Juanita. <u>Juan tiene cinco (5) años</u> y Juanita tiene siete (7) años. Vamos a comer hamburguesas y patatas fritas porque son deliciosas, y <u>por la tarde</u> vamos a jugar al tenis <u>en el parque</u> porque hacer deporte es bueno para <u>la salud</u>. Tenemos raquetas nuevas

Next weekend I'm going to go to work by car. I am a Spanish teacher and I usually work in the morning at the weekend. What a pain! I am going to work for three hours and then I'm going to go shopping and return home to make the lunch for my children, Juan and Juanita. Juan is 5 and Juanita is 7. We are going to eat hamburgers and chips because they are delicious, and in the afternoon, we are going to play tennis in the park because doing sport is good for your (the) health. We have new racquets.

See if you can remember how you say in Spanish

1. In the morning
2. In the afternoon
3. Next weekend
4. I'm going to go home
5. In order to prepare
6. For my children
7. Juan is 5 (has 5 years)
8. Juanita is 7 (has 7 years)
9. I am a teacher (I am teacher)
10. Because it is good (no word for *it*!)

Answers

1. Por la mañana
2. Por la tarde
3. El próximo fin de semana
4. Voy a volver a casa
5. Para preparar
6. Para mis hijos
7. Juan tiene cinco años
8. Juanita tiene siete años
9. Soy profesora
10. Porque es bueno

Now have a go at writing your own plans for next weekend, or even next year "el año que viene". Imagine your perfect future. What are you going to do, play, watch, where are you going to, go, live etc?

_____
_____
_____
_____
_____
_____
_____
_____
_____
_____

Dialogue 2

Pilar habla con Juan Carlos. Quiere saber si Juan Carlos tiene pasatiempos, y si tiene planes para el próximo fin de semana.

P: ¿Juan Carlos, te gusta limpiar coches? Tengo dos coches.

JC: No me gusta limpiar. No me gusta ayudar. ¿Tengo que limpiar? ¿Tengo que ayudar? Los hombres no limpian, Pilar.

P: ¿Tienes pasatiempos?

JC: Si, por la mañana me gusta jugar al voleibol en la playa con mis amigos, y por la tarde suelo ver la televisión y dormir, comer pizza, fumar y beber vino. ¿Y tu?

P: Suelo ir al gimnasio por la tarde si tengo el tiempo. Suelo volver a las cinco. Me gusta preparar comida deliciosa porque es importante comer bien.

JC: Perfecto. Me gusta la comida deliciosa.

P: ¡Que perfecto! ¿Tienes planes para el próximo fin de semana?

JC: No suelo limpiar. No suelo ayudar. No puedo preparar comida deliciosa. No me gusta ir al gimnasio. Voy a ver la tele en tu casa. Quiero comer tu comida deliciosa, voy a fumar, beber vino y dormir.

P: Tengo que volver a casa inmediatamente para preparar la comida. Voy a preparar tapas, tortilla, paella, pollo con patatas fritas y una ensalada verde.

Translation of dialogue 2

Pilar talks to Juan Carlos. She wants to know if he has hobbies and if he has plans for next weekend.

P: Juan Carlos, do you like cleaining cars? I have two cars.

JC: I don't like cleaning. I don't like helping. Do I have to clean? Do I have to help? Men don't clean, Pilar!

P: Do you have hobbies?

JC: Yes, in the morning I like to play volleyball on the beach with my friends and in the afternoon, I usually watch television, sleep, eat pizza, smoke and drink wine. What about you?

P: I usually go to the gym in the afternoon if I have the time. I usually get home at 5 o'clock. I like to prepare delicious food because it is important to eat well.

JC: Perfect. I like delicious food.

P: How perfect! Do you have plans for next weekend?

JC: I'm not accustomed to cleaning. I'm not accustomed to helping. I can't make delicious food and I don't like going to the gym. I'm going to watch television in your house. I want to eat your delicious food, smoke, drink wine and sleep.

P: I've got to go home immediately to prepare the food. I'm going to make tapas, tortilla, paella, chicken and chips and a green salad.

Recap day 2

1. You can use infinitives to avoid conjugating verbs:
   Suelo, puedo, quiero, tengo que, me gusta, voy a etc

2. Talking about the future, use *voy a* when talking about yourself, but remember to conjugate the verb: *voy, vas, va, vamos, vais, van*

3. You *have* your age, so tengo ….. años – and the he / she form of this is *tiene*.

4. As well as having your age, remember tengo que = I have to

New phrases – day 1 and 2

jugar al tenis	to play tennis
ir al cine	to go to the cinema
ir a la playa	to go to the beach
hablar con	to talk to (with)
ver la tele	to watch tv
escuchar música	to listen to music
para	for / in order to
el próximo fin de semana	next weekend
por la mañana	in the morning
por la tarde	in the afternoon
porque es	because it is
soy profesora	I am a teacher
hay	there is
tengo dos hijos	I have two children
hablar	to speak (think blah blah)
ayudar	to help (take out the u and get ayd)
llegar	to arrive (on your legs)
salir	to go out (with Sally)
volver	to return (revolving doors)
comer	to eat (come 'ere to eat)
tocar	to touch or play (toc toc toc)
sacar	to take (out of the sack)
tengo que volver	I have to return
tiene diez años	S/he is ten years old

Day 3 The past tense (the perfect tense)

If we're not talking about the future, we're usually talking about the past, telling people what we've done and asking what they have done. Examples in English are: *I went, I did, I ate, I watched.* In each of these cases there is an equivalent that grammarians call the "perfect" tense (eg. I have been, I have done, I have eaten, I have watched). It is the perfect tense that we are going to tackle here. The more complex one (the preterite) is for later and NOT covered here, except to say that fui = I went and fue = it was.

The structure of the perfect tense, equivalent to the English "I have eaten" is made up of a person (*I*), an auxiliary ("have") and a past participle ("eaten"). The auxiliary ("have") is not the verb *tener*, but another verb (haber) used specifically to make this tense. The past participle is made by removing the ar/er/ir and adding -ado or -ido to the verb.

Here's what the perfect tense looks like, taking the three types of verb in turn.

NB You will see that -ar verbs go to -ado and that -er and -ir verbs both go the same way - *ido*.

hablar	**comer**	**vivir**
he hablado	he comido	he vivido
has hablado	has comido	has vivido
ha hablado	ha comido	ha vivido
hemos hablado	hemos comido	hemos vivido
habéis hablado	habéis comido	habéis vivido
han hablado	han comido	han vivido
I have spoken	*I have eaten*	*I have lived*
You have spoken	*You have eaten*	*You have lived*
S/he has spoken	*S/he has eaten*	*S/he has lived*
We have spoken	*We have eaten*	*We have lived*
You have spoken	*You have eaten*	*You have lived*
They have spoken	*They have eaten*	*They have lived*

The past tense in practice

On the next page is a dual language dialogue showing a bossy person and their victim in action, using the past tense to find out what has been achieved today. If there are two of you, you can read it together.

First, some vocabulary

una manzana	an apple (man – Adam's apple?)
la cena	dinner
comprar	to buy
sacar fotos	to take photos
el museo	museum
nuevo	new
la bolsa	bag
tostadas	toast
mantequilla	butter ("meant to kill ya")
una naranja	an orange (a "norange")
pollo	chicken
verduras	vegetables (from "verde" – Green)
pan	bread
leer un periódico	to read a newspaper
una revista	a magazine (review)
palabras	words
la iglesia	the church
también	also
un montón de	loads of (a mountain of)
la carta	the letter
la mesa	the table
la poesía	poetry
todo / toda / todos / todas	all (ending varies with noun)
todo el tiempo	all the time
todos los días	every day
toda la tarde	all afternoon
todas las chicas	all the girls
ir de compras	
he hido de compras	

SPANISH

¿Qué has comido hoy?
He comido unas manzanas, cereales, tostadas y mucho chocolate.
¿Has ido de compras?
Sí, he ido al supermercado para comprar la cena.
¿Has comprado el pan?
Sí, he comprado las naranjas y la mantequilla también.
¿Has preparado la cena?
Sí, he preparado el pollo y las verduras.
¿Has visitado el museo?
Sí, y he visitado la iglesia y las galerías también.
¿Has sacado fotos para Instagram?
Sí, he sacado muchos selfis para mis amigos.
¿Has leído el periódico?
Sí, he leído el periódico, las revistas, el diccionario y dos libros.
¿Has aprendido las nuevas palabras españolas?
Sí, he aprendido todas las palabras.

These sentences below show you a few irregular participles in action – visto (from ver, to see), hecho (from hacer, to do), dicho (from decir, to say), vuelto (from volver, to return) and escrito (from escribir, to write).

¿Has visto mi bolsa?
Sí, he visto tu bolsa en la mesa.

¿Has hecho tus deberes?
Sí, he hecho mis deberes, he puesto la mesa y he ordenado la casa.

¿Has escrito la carta?
Sí, he escrito dos cartas, tres postales y un montón de poesía.

¿Ha vuelto? ¿Qué ha dicho?
Nada.

ENGLISH

What have you eaten today?
I have eaten some apples, cereal, toast and lots of chocolate.
Have you been shopping?
Yes, I went to the supermarket to buy the dinner.
Have you bought the bread?
Yes, I bought oranges and butter as well.
Have you made the dinner?
Yes, I have made the chicken and vegetables.
Have you visited the museum?
Yes, and I have visited the church and the galleries as well.
Have you taken photos for Instagram?
Yes, I've taken lots of selfies for my friends.
Have you read the newspaper?
Yes, I've read the newspaper, the magazines, the dictionary and two books.
Have you learnt the new Spanish words?
Yes, I've learnt all the words.

Have you seen my bag?
Yes, I saw your bag on the table.

Have you done your homework?
Yes, I have done my homework, laid the table and tidied the house.

Have you written the letter?
Yes, I've written two letters, three postcards and loads of poetry.

Has he returned? What did he say?
Nothing.

Past tense practice – read and translate back and forth

He hecho todo. He jugado al tenis, he limpiado la casa, he ido al trabajo, he hablado con mi madre, he comprado la comida, he preparado la cena, he ayudado a mis hijos con sus deberes, he leído el periódico, he escrito una carta y he visitado un museo. ¿Que has hecho? No has hecho nada.

Notice the double negative in the last sentence. "You have not done nothing"

I have done everything. I have played tennis, I have cleaned the house, I have been to work, I have talked to (with) my mother, I have bought the food, made (prepared) the dinner, helped my children with their homework, read the newspaper, written a letter and visited a museum. What have you done? You haven't done anything.

Can you write about what you have done today? Use *hablar, comer, hacer, ver, trabajar, visitar, preparar, comprar, jugar, ayudar* If you can, add what you are going to do next weekend.

_____

_____

_____

_____

_____

_____

_____

_____

_____

_____

Dialogue 3

Dos semanas más tarde, y la situación es imposible. Pilar esta triste porque piensa que Juan Carlos es un poco perezoso y egoísta. Pilar ha hecho todo. Juan Carlos no ha hecho nada. Juan Carlos no va a hacer nada. No ha salido de la casa de Pilar.

Ha comido comida deliciosa todos los días, ha fumado, ha bebido todo el vino, ha visto todos los programas en la tele, ha dormido mucho, y no ha dicho gracias. Pilar ha vuelto a casa y ha visto las botellas de vino, los cigarrillos, y no ha dicho nada. Juan Carlos ha empezado con una pregunta muy molesta.

JC: ¿Pilar, qué has hecho hoy?

P: Muchísimo. ¡Estoy muy cansada!

JC: ¿Has ido de compras?

P: Sí, he ido al supermercado para comprar la cena.

JC: ¿Has comprado el pan?

P: Sí, he comprado las naranjas y la mantequilla también.

JC: ¿Has preparado la cena?

P: Sí, he preparado el pollo y las verduras.

JC: ¿Has leído el periódico?

P: Sí, he leído el periódico, las revistas, el diccionario y dos libros. ¿Y tú?

JC: Me gusta ver la tele, dormir, comer, beber y fumar. No suelo preparar comida deliciosa, no quiero leer, no voy a comprar pan. No me gusta limpiar. No voy a ayudar. No puedo ir al gimnasio.

Did you notice that we are now saying "estoy" for "I am" whereas before we learnt "soy". In the next chapter we look at why this is....

Translation of dialogue 3

Two weeks later and the situation is impossible. Pilar is sad because she thinks that Juan Carlos is a bit lazy and selfish. She has done everything. Juan Carlos has done nothing. Juan Carlos is not going to do anything. Juan Carlos has not left Pilar's house.

He has eaten delicious food every day, he has smoked, he has drunk all the wine, he has seen all the programmes on television, he has slept a lot and he hasn't said thank you. Pilar has come home, has seen the bottles of wine and the cigarettes and hasn't said anything. Juan Carlos has begun, with a very annoying question.

JC: Pilar, what have you done today?

P: Loads. I'm very tired!

JC: Have you been shopping?

P: Yes, I have been to the supermarket to buy the dinner.

JC: Have you bought the bread?

P: Yes, I have bought oranges and butter as well.

JC: Have you made dinner?

P: Yes, I have made chicken and vegetables.

JC: Have you read the paper?

P: Yes, I have read the paper, the magazines, the dictionary and two books. What about you?

JC: I like watching television, sleeping, eating, drinking and smoking. I don't usually make delicious food, I don't want to read, I'm not going to buy bread. I don't like cleaning. I'm not going to help. I can't go to the gym.

Recap day 3

The past tense is formed in the style of "I have somethinged", where the "have" is a form of *haber* which is not the normal "to have" verb, but one used specifically for this purpose. The "somethinged", or the past participle, is formed by turning the ar into ado and the er or ir into ido.

The more complex past tense is called the preterite, and we don't cover it in this book, because it is highly irregular and time-consuming to learn!

New vocab from day 1-3

bailar	to dance (ballet)
limpiar	to clean (imagine limping afterwards)
trabajar	to work (go to a lot of trouble)
vender	to sell (vending machine)
ver	to watch (a very good programme)
beber	to drink (baby drinks milk)
viajar	to travel (voyage)
recibir	to receive (b = v)
por la tarde	in the afternoon / evening
porque es	because it is
soy	I am
hay	there is
tengo	I have
he hecho	I have done
he jugado	I have played
he comprado	I have bought
he limpiado	I have cleaned
he visto	I have seen
he escrito	I have written
he dicho	I have said
he vuelto	I have returned
he puesto	I have put
fui	I went
fue	it was
molesto	annoying
una pregunta	a question
estoy cansado	I'm tired (masculine)
estoy cansada	I'm tired (feminine)

Day 4 - *to be, to have* and *there is*

We learned on day 2 that the verb *to be* is *ser*. The great news is, there are in fact *two* verbs for *to be* – one is indeed *ser*, and the other is *estar*. You use **ser to describe the characteristics** of a thing or person, and **estar to describe states of emotion and position**. Most of the time, estar will be used with temporary states, to describe feelings and where someone or something currently is. However, that is not a hard and fast rule as the house is not going to move from where it is, and certain "emotional" states can well be permanent, such as casado (married) and divorciado (divorced).

Here are the verbs conjugated in full:

ser (characteristic)	estar (emotion / position)	
soy	estoy	I am
eres	estás	you (s) are
es	está	he, she, it is
somos	estamos	we are
sois	estáis	you are
son	están	they are

Here are some examples of their use:

¿Dónde está el hotel?	Where is the hotel?
¿Tu hermano es simpático?	Is your brother nice?
La casa es muy grande (chara.)	The house is very big
La casa está en Londres (position)	The house is in London
La casa está sucia (currently)	The house is dirty
La cocina está limpia (currently)	The kitchen is clean
El hombre es timido (chara.)	The man is shy
El hombre está casado ("emotion")	The man is married
Los gatos están contentos (emotion)	The cats are happy
Somos importantes (chara.)	We are important
Estamos divorciados ("emotion")	We are divorced
No es importante (chara.)	It/he/she's not important
Los gatos son negros (chara.)	The cats are black
Están en el jardín (position)	They are in the garden
No estoy cansado (emotion)	I'm not tired
Esta furiosa (emotion)	S/he is furious

Adjectives that go with ser

grande / pequeño	big / small
alto	tall
bajo	short
nuevo	new
antiguo / histórico / viejo	old
guapo	good-looking
joven	young
turístico	touristy
animado	lively
tímido	shy
divertido	fun
aburrido / interesante	boring / interesting
importante	important
inteligente	intelligent
bueno	good
malo	bad
gordo	fat
delgado	thin
español / inglés	Spanish / English

Adjectives that go with estar

casado	married
separado	separated
divorciado	divorced
contento	happy
enfadado	angry
cansado	tired
furioso	furious
estresado	stressed

Positions with estar

en casa	at home
en Londres / España	In London / Spain
cerca de	near
lejos de	far from
delante de	in front of
detrás de	behind
al lado de	next to
debajo de	under

An extra use of estar – to say what you *are doing*

More fantastic midweek news. Unlike French, Spanish allows you to say that you are *in the process of* doing something as well as that you do it. You can say *I'm eating*, as well as *I eat*. This is what we call the present continuous, and it is really easy to recognise:

Estoy hablando	I am talking
Estás escuchando	you are listening
Está jugando	s/he is playing
Estoy buscando	I'm looking for
Estamos trabajando	we are working
Estáis limpiando	you are cleaning
Están comiendo	they are eating
Estoy bebiendo	I am drinking
Estoy aprendiendo	I am learning
Están viendo la tele	they are watching TV
Estoy limpiando	I am cleaning
Estamos reciclando	we are recycling
Estamos comunicando	we are communicating
Estáis preparando	you (pl) are preparing
Está nadando	s/he is swimming
Está cantando	s/he is singing
Estamos esperando	we are waiting
No estoy esperando	I'm not waiting
Está durmiendo	s/he is sleeping

The last one, "durmiendo" is odd because it comes from the verb "dormir" and undergoes a change of vowel.

To summarise, we use *ser* with permanent characteristics, and *estar* with emotion, position, temporary states, and with verbs in the -ando / -iendo form to make the present continuous. It makes sense, because what you are doing at the moment could be said to be your current position. It's temporary. It's not a permanent characteristic.

Practice with ser and estar

1. I am preparing the dinner
2. I am cleaning the house
3. We are watching the television
4. The house is very dirty
5. The car is clean
6. The man is boring
7. My brother is very tall
8. The museum is boring
9. They are married
10. We are divorced
11. She is tired
12. I am at home
13. They are in London
14. They are Spanish
15. The girls are cross
16. The boys are furious
17. The hotel is near the station
18. The museum is a long way from the station
19. The station is big
20. The town is small

Answers

1. Estoy preparando la cena
2. Estoy limpiando la casa
3. Estamos viendo la television
4. La casa está muy sucia
5. El coche está limpio
6. El hombre es aburrido
7. Mi hermano es muy grande
8. El museo es aburrido
9. Están casados
10. Estamos divorciados
11. Está cansada
12. Estoy en casa
13. Están en Londres
14. Son españoles
15. Las chicas están enfadadas
16. Los chicos están furiosos
17. El hotel está cerca de la estación
18. El museo está lejos de la estación
19. La estación es grande
20. La ciudad es pequeña

If you got any wrong, go back and do them again at the end of this chapter. The correct use of these two verbs will make you sound well an truly Spanish!

Hay – there is

We met the word *hay,* pronounced "I" back on day one. You will be pleased to know that *hay* means "there is" as well as "there are". To say that *there isn't* or *there aren't* just say "no hay" and go straight to the noun – don't add un / una. If there isn't any of it, there isn't an article either.

Examples of the use of "hay"

Hay mucho tráfico en Londres	There is lots of traffic in London
No hay biblioteca en mi pueblo	There is no library in my village
Hay unos libros en la mesa	There are some books on the table
No hay sellos?	Aren't there any stamps?
Hay un perro en mi jardín	There is a dog in my garden
No hay leche en el café	There is no milk in the coffee

Write a few lines about what there is and isn't in your town – use the vocabulary section at the back to find useful words

……………………………………………………………………
……………………………………………………………………
……………………………………………………………………
……………………………………………………………………
……………………………………………………………………
……………………………………………………………………
……………………………………………………………………
……………………………………………………………………

Tener – to have

After that little brain break, there is one more thing to learn today.

We know we can use the infinitive to keep things simple, slotting it in after one of the expressions we learnt on day 2:

Suelo tener	I usually have
Me gusta tener	I like having
Puedo tener	I can have
Quiero tener	I want to have
Voy a tener	I am going to have

You might even remember how to do the past tense of tener using the rules we learnt on day 3:

He tenido	I had / have had
Has tenido	you (s) had / have had
Ha tenido	he, she, it had / has had
Hemos tenido	we had / have had
Habéis tenido	you (pl) had / have had
Han tenido	they had / have had

You may also remember using tengo = I have and tiene = he or she has (remember juan and Juanita "having" 5 and 7 years?)

Here it is in full in the present tense

Tengo	I have
Tienes	you (s) have
Tiene	he, she, it has
Temenos	we have
Tenéis	you (pl) have
Tienen	they have

And don't forget that by adding *que* you turn *have* into *have to*

Tengo que dormir	I have to sleep
No tienen que ver la tele	They don't have to watch TV
Tienes que ir?	Do you have to go?

Dialogue 4

JC: ¿Qué estás haciendo?

P: ¿Estoy limpiando la casa, y tú?

JC: Nada. Estoy en el sofá, viendo la tele.

P: ¿Quieres ayudar?

JC: No gracias, estoy contento aquí. No me gusta ayudar. Hay un programa muy interesante que quiero ver.

P: Vale.

JC: Tengo hambre. Quiero comer. ¿Qué tienes?

P: No mucho. Hay solo pan y mantequilla, unas manzanas y cereales.

JC: ¿Quieres salir a comprar una pizza?

P: No mucho, pero si quieres una pizza…

JC: Hay pizzas deliciosas en el supermercado. Tienes que ir al supermercado.

P: Hay pan delicioso en la cocina, y mantequilla deliciosa, manzanas deliciosas y cereales deliciosos.

JC: No quiero comer tu comida. Quiero comer pizza.

P: Eres muy difícil. No tengo que comprar pizza.

JC: No, tú eres perezosa y egoísta porque no quieres comprar pizza para tu marido.

P: No. Soy muy generosa y paciente y simpática.

JC: Afortunadamente, soy paciente también. Puedo esperar.

P: Muchas gracias.

JC: Unos minutos, no más.

Translation of Dialogue 4

JC: What are you doing?

P: Cleaning the house. And you?

JC: Nothing. I'm on the sofa watching TV

P: Do you want to help?

JC: No thank you I am happy here. I don't like helping. There is a very interesting programme I want to watch.

P: Okay.

JC: I'm hungry. I want to eat. What have you got?

P: Not much. There's only bread and cheese, some apples and cereal.

JC: Do you want to go out and buy a pizza?

P: Not much. But if you want a pizza...

JC: There are delicious pizzas in the supermarket. You have to go to the supermarket.

P: There is delicious bread in the kitchen, and delicious butter, delicious apples and delicious cereal.

JC: I don't want to eat your food. I want to eat pizza.

P: You are very difficult. I don't have to buy pizza.

JC: No, you are lazy and selfish because you don't want to buy pizza for your husband.

P: No, I am very generous and patient and nice.

JC: Fortunately, I am also patient. I can wait.

P: Thank you very much.

JC: A few minutes, not more.

Recap day 4

Ser is used as the verb *to be* when you are talking about the permanent qualities or characteristics of a person, place or thing. It goes like this: *soy, eres, es, somos, sois, son.*

Estar is used as the verb *to be* when you are talking about the emotional state of a person (including their marital state) or the position of a person, place or thing. It goes like this: *estoy, estás, está, estamos, estáis, están.*

Estar can be used with the *-ing* version of the verb, which in Spanish ends with *-ando* or *-iendo,* to express what you are actually doing currently. This is called the present continuous.

Hay means *there is* or *there are* and if you want to say that there isn't any of something, you don't use the article. So, *no hay* means *there is no* and is never followed by *un, una, unos* or *unas*

Tener means *to have* and *tener que* means *to have to.* It has an unusual conjugation: *tengo, tienes, tiene, tenemos, tenéis, tienen.*

Ser, estar, hay, tener

La casa está muy sucia	The house is very dirty
El coche está limpio	The car is clean
El hombre es aburrido	The man is boring
Mi hermano es alto	My brother is tall
No hay sellos?	Aren't there any stamps?
No hay leche	There is no milk
Tengo que dormir	I have to sleep
Tienes que ir?	Do you have to go?
Tiene veinte años	She is 20
He tenido un accidente	I have had an accident
Estamos divorciados	We are divorced

Recap vocabulary days 1-4

esperar	to wait for / hope (going spare!)
buscar	to look for (a bus or a car)
pensar en	to think about (tapping a pen on your head thinking)
olvidar	to forget (forget about Olly)
comprender	to understand (comprehend)
aprender	to learn (apprentice)
compartir	to share (divide into compartments)
para	for / in order to
por la tarde	in the afternoon / evening
porque es	because it is
soy	I am
hay	there is
tengo	I have
he hecho	I have done
he visto	I have seen
he escrito	I have written
he dicho	I have said
he preparado	I have prepared
he olvidado	I have forgotten
voy a pensar	I am going to think
vamos a ir	we are going to go
estoy	I am (position / emotion)
está	he, she, it is (position / emotion)
estamos	we are (position / emotion)
están	they are (position / emotion)
es	he, she, it is (characteristic)
somos	we are (characteristic)
son	they are (characteristic)
tengo	I have
tiene que	he, she, it has to
tenemos	we have
tienen	they have
he tenido	I have had
hemos ido	we have gone
han ido	they have gone

NOTES

Day 5 - liking and pronouns

Expressing liking, using the verb *gustar*

Me gusta bail**ar**	I like dancing
No me gusta nada limpi**ar**	I don't like cleaning at all
Me gusta el perro	I like the dog
Me gusta**n los perros**	I like dog**s**
No me gusta**n** nada **las manzanas**	I don't like apple**s** at all
Le gusta comer	S/he likes eating
A mi hermano le gusta beber	My brother likes drinking

What do you observe here?

- Firstly, the structure is *"to me pleases X"* rather than *"I like X"*.

- Secondly, there is no -ing after the like verb. Use an infinitive instead.

- Thirdly, when the thing that you like is plural, you add an *n* to the liking verb. Where there's an *s* there's an *n*...

- To add a complication, if someone else likes something, we have to change the pronoun *me* to te, le, nos, os, or les

Me gusta(n) *add n if the thing you like is plural*	I like
Te gusta(n)	you (s) like
Le gusta(n)	he/she likes
Nos gusta(n)	we like
Os gusta(n)	you (pl) like
Les gusta(n)	they like

- If we are naming the person who likes the thing, then add A just before their name.

A Fred le gusta bailar	Fred likes dancing
A Doris le gusta el chocolate	Doris likes chocolate
A mi hermana le gustan los gatos	My sister likes cats
A mis amigas les gusta el perro	My friends like the dog
A mis hermanos les gusta comer	My brothers like eating
A mis amigos les gustan los caramelos	My friends like sweets

The crucial point to note is that the thing you like is the subject of the sentence. That's why the verb *gustar* changes if the thing you like is plural. The think you like *governs* the verb gustar; and that is also why you need to include the article el / la / los / las before the noun in each case. In English you can say "I like chocolate", in Spanish you need to say "me pleases the chocolate".

Practise using the verb gustar – to like

1. I like dogs
2. I like Madrid
3. She likes cats
4. We like chocolate
5. They like apples
6. I don't like London
7. She doesn't like elephants
8. We don't like bread
9. My brother doesn't like cleaning
10. Juan Carlos doesn't like preparing food

1. Me gustan los perros
2. Me gusta Madrid
3. Le gustan los gatos
4. Nos gusta el chocolate
5. Les gustan las manzanas
6. No me gusta Londres
7. No le gustan los elefantes
8. No nos gusta el pan
9. A mi hermano lo le gusta limpiar
10. A Juan Carlos no le gusta preparar la comida

Using pronouns as direct objects (*eg. I see him / she sees me*)

Look at the verb ver = to see

veo	I see
ves	you (s) see
ve	he / she / it sees
vemos	we see
veis	you (pl) see
ven	they see

We can put personal pronouns in front of verbs (where in English they come after the verb)

To say he sees me	Me ve (the "me" comes first)
To say you (s) see me	Me ves
To say they see me	Me ven

And it's not just me, it's you! (or him, her, it, us, them…)

Lo veo	I see him (or it, with a masculine noun)
La veo	I see her (or it, with a feminine noun)
Los veo	I see them (masculine)
Las veo	I see them (feminine)
Nos ven	They see us
Nos ves	You (s) see us
Nos ve	He / she sees us
Lo vemos	We see him (or it, with a masculine noun)
La vemos	We see her (or it, with a feminine noun)
Los vemos	We see them (masculine)
Las vemos	We see them (feminine)
Lo como	I eat it (eg. el chocolate)
La como	I eat it (eg. la pizza)
Los como	I eat them (eg. los caramelos)
Las como	I eat them (eg. las fresas)
La bebo	I drink it (eg. la cerveza)
Lo / la odio	I hate it
Lo estudio	I study it
Las conozco	I know them (eg. las chicas)
Lo he comido	I have eaten it
Las he visto	I have seen them

Pronouns on the end of verbs

After an infinitive, or a gerund (which is the -ando -iendo ending), you can actually stick the pronoun on the end.

No me gusta verlo	I don't like seeing him / it
Quiero comerlos	I want to eat them
Suelen ayudarnos	They usually help us
Voy a beberla	I'm going to drink it (feminine)
Van a comprarlas	They are going to buy them
Va a ayudarme	He / she is going to help me.
Estoy comiendolo	I'm eating it

Here's a passage in Spanish using a variety of expressions we have covered in the last five days: It's written by Pedro, Pilar's son, who is a bit put out by the arrival of Juan Carlos.

Me gustan los fines de semana porque no tengo que estudiar y puedo dormir mucho. Suelo ir al supermercado con mi madre para comprar comida deliciosa. Hoy voy a comprarla y vamos a prepararla en la cocina. A mi madre le gusta Juan Carlos. No me gusta nada. Cuando no hay pizza, no está contenta. A Juan Carlos le gusta beber vino. Lo bebe por la mañana y por la tarde también. Le gusta beberlo. Está siempre bebiéndolo. Voy a decir a mi madre que no me gusta su novio. Voy a decirlo hoy.

I like weekends because I don't have to study and I can sleep a lot. I usually go to the supermarket with my mother to buy delicious food. Today I'm going to buy it and we are going to prepare it in the kitchen. My mother likes Juan Carlos. I don't like him at all. When there isn't any pizza, he is not happy. Juan Carlos likes drinking wine. He drinks it in the morning and in the afternoon as well. He likes drinking it. He is always drinking it. I am going to tell my mother I don't like her boyfriend. I'm going to say it today.

Notice that *I don't like him* is *no me gusta.* You don't have to mention him at all, because *he* or *el* is one of those optional subject pronouns we talked about on Day 1. You could equally say "El no me gusta" or "No me gusta Juan Carlos"

Dialogue 5

Pilar habla con su hijo. Su hijo no está contento. No quiere vivir con Juan Carlos. Piensa que Juan Carlos es perezoso y egoista. Pilar no ha pensado mucho en su hijo. Esta triste porque su hijo está triste. Afortunadamente Juan Carlos es en el dormitorio porque le gusta dormir.

Pedro: Hay un problema Mama, No me gusta Juan Carlos.

Pilar: ¿Por qué? No comprendo.

Pedro: No me gusta porque es egoísta y perezoso.

Pilar: ¿Qué?

Pedro: No le gusta ayudar en casa, le gusta solo dormir, comer, beber y fumar. Es maleducado.

Pilar: ¿Piensas que es maleducado?

Pedro: Si, pienso. He decidido que no quiero vivir aquí. Voy a buscar un apartamento en la ciudad.

Pilar: No, Pedro, por favor. Voy a hablar con Juan Carlos.

Pedro: No va a cambiar.

Pilar: No, pero tiene un hijo que vive en Madrid.

Pedro: Tiene que ir a vivir con su hijo.

Pilar: Vamos a ver

Pedro: Gracias Mama.

Translation of Dialogue 5

Pilar is talking to her son. Her son is not happy. He doesn't want to live with Juan Carlos. He thinks that Juan Carlos is lazy and selfish. Pilar hasn't thought much about her son. She is sad because her son is sad. Fortunately, Juan Carlos is in the bedroom because he likes sleeping.

Pedro: There is a problem Mum. I don't like Juan Carlos.

Pilar: Why not? I don't understand.

Pedro: I don't like him because he is selfish and lazy.

Pilar: What?

Pedro: He doesn't like helping at home. He only likes sleeping, eating, drinking and smoking. He is rude.

Pilar: Do you think he is rude?

Pedro: Yes, I think so. I have decided that I don't want to live here. I am going to look for an apartment in the city.

Pilar: No Pedro, please. I'm going to talk to Juan Carlos.

Pedro: He won't change.

Pilar: No, but he has a son who lives in Madrid.

Pedro: He has to go and live with his son.

Pilar: We shall see.

Pedro: Thanks, Mum.

Recap day 5

1. Liking is a special case when it comes to verbs in Spanish. The thing that you like is the subject of the verb *gustar*, and is either an infinitive, or if a noun, must always be preceded by a definite article (el, la, los, las)
2. This means that if you like something that is plural, *gusta* gets an -n (*me gustan los perros*)
3. If someone else likes something, use *te, le, nos, os or les* before the *gusta*.
4. *Me gusta* means *I like it* as well as *I like* – no need to put any kind of "it" on the end. Ditto with me gustan – I like, or I like them. No need to add any kind of "them" in Spanish to match the English.
5. Direct object pronouns come before the noun, but can be added on the end of an infinitive or a gerund. So *me ve* means *He sees me* but *quiero verlos* means *I want to see them*.

New vocab reminder

Me gusta el chocolate	I like chocolate
Me gustan los caramelos	I like sweets
A Pedro no le gusta el chocolate	Pedro doesn't like chocolate
No le gustan los perros	He doesn't like dogs
Le gusta jugar al tenis	He likes playing tennis
Les gusta la pizza	They like pizza
No les gustan los coches	They don't like cars
No quiero verlo	I don't want to see him / it
No suelo hacerlo	I don't usually do it
No voy a comerlos	I'm not going to eat them
Los veo	I see them
La como	I eat it (a feminine thing)
Las he comido	I have eaten them (f pl)
Voy a comerlos	I'm going to eat them (m pl)

NOTES

Day 6 - reflexives and the verb *hacer (to do)*
Reflexive verbs

These exist in most languages except English. They exist to express things that you do to *yourself* ie. shower, wash, brush teeth, wake up and get up. You can shower (duchar) someone else, or you can shower yourself (duchar**se**). You can wash something or someone else (lavar) or wash yourself (lavar**se**). You can lift up something (levantar) or get yourself up out of bed (levantarse). If you want to use these verbs in the I form, in any tense just put *me* on the front (pronounced *"meh"* not *"me"*).

Me levanto	I get up
Me he levantado	I got up
Me voy a levantar	I'm going to get up

So *me* means *me* – as in I get me (myself) up.

Me ducho	from ducharse	I shower
Me lavo	from lavarse	I wash (myself)
Me acuesto	from acostarse	I go to bed
Me visto	from vestirse	I get dressed
Me divierto	from divertirse	I have fun
Me quedo	from quedarse	I stay
Me relajo	from relajarse	I relax
Me bronceo	from broncearse	I sunbathe

Here's how it goes when it's other people doing it:

Me levanto	I get up
Te levantas	you get up
Se levanta	he / she gets up
Nos levantamos	we get up
Os levantáis	you (pl) get up
Se levantan	they get up

And in other tenses
Voy a levantarme	I am going to get up
Me he levantado	I have got up
Me he duchado	I have showered

Hacer = to do / make (remember it sounds like "athair")

Just like its equivalent in French, this verb plays a very important role in many areas. Here it is in the present tense:

hago	I do / make
haces	you (s) do / make
hace	he / she does / make
hacemos	we do / make
hacéis	you (pl) do / make
hacen	they do / make

In the future, just use the infinitive hacer after the verb "ir"

voy a hacer	I will do / make
vas a hacer	you (s) will do / make
va a hacer	he / she will do / make
vamos a hacer	we will do / make
vais a hacer	you (pl) will do / make
van a hacer	they will do / make

In the past, remember this one has an irregular past participle

he hecho	I have done / made
has hecho	you have done / made
ha hecho	he / she has done / made
hemos hecho	we have done / made
habéis hecho	you (pl) have done / made
han hecho	they have done / made

The reason it is so important is that we need to know how to use it with set expressions. Most of the time, you can translate "do" by "hacer" but you can't always do the reverse. So if you see a form of the verb hacer, you may have to think before jumping to conclusions.

On the next page is a list of the main ways this verb is used.

When to use *hacer*

For things you do or make
Hago mis deberes	I do my homework
Hago natación	I swim / go swimming
Hago vela	I sail / go sailing
Hago esquí	I ski / go skiing
Hago deporte	I do sport
Hago mi cama	I make my bed
Hago un pastel	I make a cake
Hago errores	I make mistakes
Hago muchas preguntas	I ask a lot of questions

To say what something makes you (happy, sad etc)
Me hace feliz	It makes me happy
Me hace enfadado	It makes me angry
Me hace furioso	It makes me furious
Me hace relajar	It makes me relax
Me hace reir	It makes me laugh

For the weather
Hace buen / mal tiempo	the weather is good / bad
Hace sol	it's sunny
Hace calor	it's hot
Hace frio	it's cold
Hace viento	it's windy

Contrast this with raining and snowing
Llueve	it's raining
Nieva	it's snowing

And to express how long ago something happened:
Hace dos años	two years ago
Hace poco	not long ago
Hace unos meses	a few months ago
Hace tres días	three days ago

Examples in all the tenses – test yourself

1. hago mis deberes — I do my homework
2. haces tus deberes — you do your homework
3. no hace nada — s/he doesn't do anything
4. estoy haciendo mis deberes — I'm doing my homework
5. no he hecho mi cama — I haven't made my bed
6. voy a hacer un pastel — I'm going to make a cake
7. he hecho muchos errores — I have made a lot of mistakes
8. hace sol — it is sunny
9. me hace reir — it makes me laugh
10. hace dos semanas — two weeks ago
11. hace poco — recently
12. va a hacer frio — it's going to be cold
13. me hace contento — it makes me happy
14. he hecho mis deberes — I have done my homework
15. estoy haciendo mi cama — I'm making my bed
16. está haciendo sus deberes — he is doing his homework
17. no hacemos deporte — we don't do sport
18. hago vela — I go sailing
19. no hace natación — he / she doesn't go swimming
20. no hemos hecho la cama — we haven't made the bed
21. están haciendo errores — they are making mistakes

Dialogue 6

Pilar y Juan Carlos están en el salón. Juan Carlos no está contento. Pilar ha decidido que no le gusta mucho Juan Carlos porque es perezoso y egoísta y no va a ayudar. Juan Carlos no quiere salir.

JC: Hace frío. No me gusta. Me gusta el sol.

P: No hace frío. Hace calor en casa.

JC: No hace suficiente calor.

P: Vale, no hace calor. Puedes ver la tele, ¿no?

JC: Me gusta ver la tele, pero no hay programas interesantes. Es aburrido.

P: ¿Qué has hecho hoy? ¿Vas a salir con tus amigos?

JC: No quiero salir con mis amigos porque hace frío y no tengo amigos. No me gustan las personas estúpidas.

P: Vale. ¿Quieres hacer tu cama?

JC: No quiero hacer mi cama porque no tengo que hacerlo y soy perezoso.

P: ¿Qué vas a hacer, entonces?

JC: Nada, como siempre.

P: ¿Quieres ir a Madrid?

JC: ¿Por qué?

P: Tu hijo Ramón vive en Madrid con su familia. Si no te gusta vivir en mi casa, puedes vivir con Ramón, ¿no?

JC: No quiero vivir con Ramón.

P: Madrid es una ciudad maravillosa. Hay museos, galerías, parques, restaurantes...

JC: No me gustan los museos. Me gusta dormir...

P: Fumar, beber, comer pizza, ver la tele...

JC: Voy a pensar, pero primero, voy a dormir.

Translation of dialogue 6

Pilar and Juan Carlos are in the lounge. Juan Carlos is not happy. Pilar has decided she doesn't like Juan Carlos much because he's lazy and selfish and won't help. Juan Carlos doesn't want to leave.

JC: It's cold. I don't like it. I like the sun.

P: It's not cold. It's warm in the house.

JC: It's not hot enough.

P: Okay, it's not hot. You can watch TV, can't you?

JC: I like watching TV but there aren't any interesting programmes. It's boring.

P: What have you done today? Are you going to go out with your friends?

JC: I don't want to go out with my friends because it's cold, and I don't have friends. I don't like stupid people.

P: Okay, do you want to make your bed?

JC: I don't want to make my bed because I don't have to do it and I am lazy.

P: What are you going to do then?

JC: Nothing, as usual.

P: Do you want to go to Madrid?

JC: Why?

P: Your son Ramon lives in Madrid with his family. If you don't like living in my house, you can live with Ramon, can't you?

JC: I don't want to live with Ramon

P: Madrid is a marvellous city. There are museums, galleries, parks, restaurants...

JC: I don't like museums. I like sleeping....

P: Smoking, drinking, eating pizza, watching television...

JC: I will have a think. But first, I am going to have a sleep.

Recap day 6

Reflexive verbs are the ones you do to yourself – get up, shower, wash, go to bed etc. They work the same as other verbs, but you put a *me* (or equivalent) in front of them.

Me levanto	I get up
Me ducho	I shower
Me acuesto	I go to bed
Me he levantado	I have got up
Voy a ducharme	I am going to have a shower
Tengo que acostarme	I've got to go to bed
Suelo levantarme	I usually get up

Hacer is a useful verb because it not only means to do or make, but can be used to say when you did something (how long ago) and to describe the weather. You DO most actitivies in Spanish (sport, swimming, sailing) whereas in English you might say *I go swimming* or *I play sport*.

Using hacer, see if you can remember how to say

I make my bed	hago mi cama
I have made my bed	he hecho mi cama
I'm going to make my bed	voy a hacer mi cama
It makes me laugh	me hace reir
It makes me angry	me hace enfadado
The weather is good	hace buen tiempo
It's hot	hace calor
I made a cake	he hecho un pastel
He is making lots of mistakes	hace muchos errores
Recently	hace poco
2 weeks ago	hace dos semanas

NOTES

Day 7 The personal *a*

I have left this till last because it's a little bit tricky to get your head around.

Firstly, you need to understand what a direct object is. If I say "I see the boy", *the boy* is the direct object of the verb *to see*. Similarly with "I help my friend", the *friend* is the direct object of the verb *to help*.

In Spanish, where the direct object of a verb is animate (ie. alive) then it must be preceded by the word *"a"*, which normally means *"to"* but in this case is just recognition of the next noun being a living thing. You might imagine this to be putting some polite distance between you and the other person, but bear in mind that it might be an animal too. If it is a masculine singular noun, you will need to condense the *"a"* and the *"el"* to form *"al"*, so you can't say *veo a el perro*, you say *veo al perro*.

Examples

veo a la chica	I see the girl
veo al perro	I see the dog
veo a mis amigas	I see my friends
veo el pan	I see the bread (inanimate)
veo las casas	I see the houses (inanimate)

Here are some verbs you might use with an animate object, requiring the personal a:

ayudar	to help
mirar	to look at
pasear	to walk (eg. dog)
odiar	to hate
animar	to encourage
escuchar	to listen to
acompañar	to accompany
conocer	to know (a person)
buscar	to look for

Don't use the personal a with tener (*tengo un hermano* NOT *a un hermano*) or with non-specific things (*busco un marido* NOT *a un marido*)

The finale – the fate of Juan Carlos is revealed...

En el café a mediodía. Entra Diego, un amigo de Ramón.

- D: ¡Hola Ramón! ¿Qué tal?
- R: Fenomenal gracias. ¿Y tu?
- D: Así así.
- R: ¿Qué pasa?
- D: No mucho. Voy a ir al supermercado para comprar comida. ¡Qué aburrido!
- R: ¡No! El supermercado es una experiencia fenomenal.
- D: ¿Quieres venir?
- R: Lo siento, pero no puedo. Mi padre va a llegar a la estación a las dos de la tarde.
- D: ¿Tu padre va a venir en tren? Pero no le gusta el tren.
- R: Quizás le gustan los trenes españoles. Vamos a ver.
- D: ¿Y qué vas a hacer con tu padre?
- R: Mañana vamos a visitar el museo. Me gustan los museos y su hotel está cerca de un museo magnifico. Después vamos a ir a un restaurante y vamos a beber mucho vino y vamos a volver a casa muy tarde, a medianoche, pienso.
- D: Excelente. Vas a estar borracho y cansado.
- R: Mi día ideal.
- D: ¿A tu padre le gusta beber? ¿Le gustan los museos? Tienes que preguntar, porque si no le gustan los museos, va a ser enfadado.
- R: Claro que sí. Va a ser un día maravilloso.
- D: Espero que sí. ¡Adiós!

In the café at midday – Diego, Ramon's friend comes in.

D: Hello Ramon, how are you?

R: Great thanks, you?

D: Not bad

R: What's happening?

D: Not much. I'm going to the supermarket to buy food. How dull!

R: No! The supermarket is a fantastic experience

D: Do you want to come?

R: Sorry but I can't. My father is arriving at the station at 2 in the afternoon.

D: Your father's coming by train? But he doesn't like the train.

R: Maybe he likes Spanish trains. We shall see.

D: Ad what are you going to do with your father?

R: Tomorrow we are going to visit the museum. I like museums and his hotel is next to a magnificent museum. Afterwards we are going to go to a restaurant and we are going to drink a lot of wine and return home very late, at midnight I think.

D: Excellent. You Will be drunk and tired.

R: My ideal day.

D: Does your father like drinking? Does he like museums? You need to ask because if he doesn't like museums he's going to be cross.

R: Of course he does. It will be a marvellous day.

D: I hope so.

R: Bye.

A la estación, a las dos de la tarde

R: ¡Hola Papa! ¿Qué tal estás?

JC: No estoy bien. No me gusta viajar en tren.

R: Pero te gustan los trenes españoles, ¿no?

JC: No me gustan nada los trenes y los trenes españoles son terribles.

R: ¡Que lástima! Vas a olvidar tu viaje porque vamos a ir al hotel en coche.

JC: No voy a olvidarlo.

R: Bueno. ¿Te gusta mi coche? Lo he comprado el fin de semana pasado.

JC: Tu coche está sucio. Tienes que limpiarlo

R: Voy a limpiarlo el próximo fin de semana

JC: ¿Dónde está el hotel?

R: No está lejos. Está en el centro cerca del museo.

JC: No me gustan los museos. El ultimo museo que he visitado fue terrible.

R: Vale. No tienes que ir al museo, Papa. No vamos a visitarlo. Vamos a visitar la galería de arte moderna. Estay muy cerca del hotel.

JC: No me gustan las galerias. La ultima galería que he visitado fue terrible también.

R: Vale. No vamos a visitarla. Aquí estamos. El hotel es lujoso. Las habitaciones son fenomenales.

JC: ¿Aquí? No me gusta. ¿Dónde están mis maletas?

R: Están en el coche, no te preocupes.

At the station at 2pm

R: Hi Dad! How are you?

JC: I'm not well. I don't like travelling by train.

R: But you like Spanish trains, no?

JC: I don't like trains at all, and Spanish trains are terrible.

R: What a pity. You will forget your journey because we will go to the hotel by car.

JC: I won't forget it.

R: Okay. Do you like my car? I bought it last weekend.

JC: Your car is dirty. You need to clean it.

R: I will clean it next weekend.

JC: Where is the hotel?

R: It's not far. It's in the centre near the museum.

JC: I don't like museums. The last museum I visited was terrible.

R: Okay. You don't have to go the museum, Dad. We won't visit it. We are going to visit the modern art gallery. It's very near the hotel.

JC: I don't like galleries. The last gallery I visited was terrible as well.

R: Okay. We won't visit it. Here we are. The hotel is luxurious. The rooms are amazing.

JC: Here? I don't like it. Where are my suitcases?

R: They are in the car. Don't worry.

JC:	¿Dónde está mi habitación?
R:	En el tercer piso.
JC:	¿Dónde está la llave?
R:	Aquí está.
JC:	¿A qué hora desayunamos?
R:	A las siete y media.
JC:	¿Y Adónde vamos a ir mañana?
R:	Vamos a visitar varios sitios turísticos en la ciudad.
JC:	No quiero visitar el museo. No quiero visitar la galería.
R:	No hay problema. No vamos a visitarlos. ¿Qué quieres hacer?
JC:	¡Voy a tener hambre! ¡Voy a necesitar comida!
R:	Vale. Vamos a comer en un restaurante en el campo y probar los platos típicos de la región.
JC:	¿A qué hora vamos a comer?
R:	A la una, como siempre. Hay un vino fenomenal que tienes que probar.
JC:	No me gusta beber alcohol. Es malo para la salud.
R:	Estupendo. No vamos a beber.
JC:	Estoy cansado.
R:	Vale. Me voy. Adiós. Hasta mañana.
JC:	Tengo que levantarme a las siete para desayunar a las siete y media. ¡Qué pena!

JC: Where is my room?

R: On the third floor.

JC: Where is the key?

R: Here it is.

JC: What time do we have breakfast?

R: At 7.30

JC: And where are we going to go tomorrow?

R: We are going to visit various tourist attractions in the city.

JC: I don't want to visit the museum. I don't want to visit the gallery.

R: No problem. We are not going to visit them. What do you want to do?

JC: I'm going to be hungry. I'm going to need food.

R: Okay. We'll eat in a restaurant in the countryside and try the local dishes.

JC: What time are we going to have lunch?

R: At 1pm, as always. There is an amazing wine which you need to try.

JC: I don't like drinking alcohol. It's bad for you.

R: Brilliant. We won't drink.

JC: I'm tired.

R: Okay, I'm going. Goodbye. Until tomorrow.

JC: I have to get up at seven to have breakfast at seven thirty. What a pain.

Juan Carlos no quiere dormir. Tiene muchos problemas con su habitación y manda un mensaje en WhatsApp:

¿Pilar, qué has hecho? No estoy bien. No me gustan nada los trenes. El viaje fue terrible. La comida fue mala. No me gusta Madrid. Hace calor. Me gusta el hotel, pero no hay piscina. Hay un jardín, pero no hay árboles. Necesito un sombrero o un parasol. En mi habitación hay una cama y un armario, pero no hay cortinas. ¿Cómo voy a dormir sin cortinas? El baño está sucio y no hay agua caliente. ¿Cómo voy a ducharme? ¡He visto una araña en el baño! Y también es muy ruidoso porque los coches en la calle hacen muchísimo ruido. Hay muchísimos problemas con el hotel. Voy a hablar con el director mañana. He tenido que pasar todo el dia con Ramon y estoy cansado y enfadado. Quiero volver a tu casa. No tengo que quedarme en Madrid.

Juan Carlos doesn't want to sleep. He has a lot of problems with his room and he sends a message on Whatsapp:

Pilar what have you done? I'm not good. I don't like trains at all. The journey was terrible. The food was bad. I don't like Madrid. It's hot. I like the hotel but there isn't a pool. There is a garden but there aren't any trees. I need a hat or a parasol. In my room there is a bed and a cupboard but there aren't any curtains. How am I going to sleep without curtains? The bathroom is dirty and there is no hot water. How am I going to shower? I have seen a spider in the bath! And also, it's very noisy because the cars in the street make a lot of noise. There are very many problems with the hotel. I will speak with the director tomorrow. I have had to spend all day with Ramon and I am tired and cross. I want to to go back to your house. I don't have to stay in Madrid.

El director del hotel ha mandado a Ramon el mensaje que ha recibido de Juan Carlos. Ramón está triste. No ha dormido toda la noche. El problema es que no le gusta su padre. No quiere admitirlo. Toma su móvil y llama a Pilar

R: ¡Hola Pilar!

P: ¿Ramón, ¿qué tal?

R: Fatal.

P: ¿Por qué?

R: No me gusta mi padre.

P: ¿Qué?

R: Es un hombre egoísta, antipático, perezoso, maleducado y estúpido.

P: Y aburrido, intolerante, arrogante...

R: No quiero pasar más tiempo con él. No quiere visitar sitios turísticos. Tiene problemas con todo. Tiene que volver a tu casa porque estoy cansado y no puedo más. Voy a ir a mi casa.

P: ¿Y Juan Carlos? ¿Qué vamos a hacer con él?

R: Es tu marido. Tienes que decidir.

P: Vamos a divorciar. He decidido que no necesito hombres para estar contenta.

R: Una decisión maravillosa.

P: ¡Celebramos!

The director of the hotel has sent the message he has received from Juan Carlos to Ramon. Ramon is sad. He hasn't slept all night. The problem is he doesn't like his father. He doesn't want to admit it. He takes his phone and phones Pilar.

R: Hello Pilar

P: Ramon, how are you?

R: Awful.

P: Why?

R: I don't like my father.

P: What?

R: He is selfish, nasty, lazy, rude and stupid.

P: And boring, intolerant and arrogant…

R: I don't want to spend any more time with him. He doesn't want to visit tourist attractions, he has problems with everything. He has to go back to your house because I'm tired and I can't do any more. I'm going to go home.

P: And Juan Carlos? What are we going to do with him?

R: He's your husband. You have to decide.

P: We will get divorced. I have decided that I don't need men to be happy.

R: A marvellous decision.

P: Let's celebrate!

Recap day 7

Go over the dialogue, firstly as Juan Carlos, then as Ramon. See if you can remember how to say:

1. Where is the hotel?
2. Where is my suitcase?
3. Where are my suitcases?
4. When do we have breakfast?
5. There is a spider in the bathroom
6. There aren't any curtains
7. I can't sleep
8. I'm exhausted
9. I'm going to need food and wine
10. I'm going to be drunk
11. I've lost my passport
12. Is there a shop where I can buy an English paper
13. It's very noisy
14. I don't like it
15. I want to go home

1. ¿Dónde está el hotel?
2. ¿Dónde está mi maleta?
3. ¿Dónde están mis maletas?
4. ¿Cuándo desayunamos?
5. Hay una araña en el bano
6. No hay cortinas
7. No puedo dormir
8. Estoy cansado / agotado
9. Voy a necesitar comida y vino
10. Voy a estar borracho
11. He perdido mi pasaporte
12. ¿Hay una tienda donde puedo comprar un periódico ingles?
13. Es muy ruidoso
14. No me gusta
15. Quiero volver a casa

NOTES

Verb tables and vocabulary

Regular verbs in the present tense

-ar **HABLAR** (to speak)	-er **COMER** (to eat)	-ir **VIVIR** (to live)
hablo	como	vivo
hablas	comes	vives
habla	come	vive
hablamos	comemos	vivimos
habláis	coméis	vivís
hablan	comen	viven
Simiilar verbs: ayudar – to help preparar – to prepare escuchar – to listen to bailar – to dance cantar – to sing limpiar – to clean trabajar – to work estudiar – to study visitar – to visit esperar – hope/ wait buscar – to look for mirar – to look at ganar – to earn, win comprar – to buy pagar – to pay (for) necesitar – to need pintar – to paint dibujar – to draw llegar – to arrive charlar – to chat cocinar – to cook contestar – to answer gastar – to spend malgastar – to waste salvar – to save mandar – to send enseñar – to teach	Similar verbs: aprender – to learn beber – to drink comprender – to understand deber – to have to esconder – to hide responder – to answer vender – to sell	Similar verbs: abolir – to abolish añadir – to add aplaudir – to applaud abrir – to open asistir a – to attend confundir – to confuse decidir – to decide definir – to define describir – to describe descubrir – to discover cubrir – to cover discutir – to discuss escribir – to write interrumpir – to interrupt prohibir – to prohibit recibir – to receive unir – to unite

Irregular and radical changing verbs in the present tense

hacer – to do	poner - to put	salir – to go out
hago	pongo	salgo
haces	pones	sales
hace	pone	sale
hacemos	ponemos	salimos
hacéis	ponéis	salís
hacen	ponen	salen
tener – to have	**venir – to come**	**empezar – to begin**
tengo	vengo	empiezo
tienes	vienes	empiezas
tiene	viene	empieza
temenos	venimos	empezamos
tenéis	venís	empezáis
tienen	vienen	empiezan
ser – to be	**estar – to be**	**ir – to go**
soy	estoy	voy
eres	estás	vas
es	está	va
somos	estamos	vamos
sois	estáis	vais
son	están	van
poder – to be able	**jugar – to play**	**volver – to return**
puedo	juego	vuelvo
puedes	juegas	vuelves
puede	juega	vuelve
podemos	jugamos	volvemos
podéis	jugáis	volvéis
pueden	juegan	vuelven
decir – to say	**dar – to give**	**pensar – to think**
digo	doy	pienso
dices	das	piensas
dice	da	piensa
decimos	damos	pensamos
decís	dais	pensáis
dicen	dan	piensan

NOTES

Vocabulary lists by topic

RELATIONSHIPS AND DESCRIBING PEOPLE

Family

en mi familia	in my family
mi padre	my father
mi madre	my mother
mis padres	my parents
mi hermano	my brother
mi hermana	my sister
mayor / menor	older / younger
soy hijo único	I'm an only child *(unique)*
mis abuelos	my grandparents
mi primo / mi prima	my cousin
mi tío	my uncle *(go for tea with him)*
mi tía	my aunt
gemelos, gemelas	twins
el hijo	son
la hija	daughter
el bebé	baby
el marido	husband *(married-o)*
la mujer / esposa	wife
el chico	boy
la chica	girl
mi hermano se llama	my brother is called
no tengo hermanos	I don't have any siblings

> *Common mistake:* **se llama** = *is called,*
> **que se llama** = *who is called*

How you get on

nos llevamos bien	we get on well
muchas cosas en común	lots of things in common
nos gustan	we like (plural thing)
los mismos programas	the same programmes
discutimos	we argue
nos gusta	we like (singular thing)
la misma música	the same music
no le gusta(n)	he / she doesn't like

86

Types of relationship and family
una relación	a relationship
enamorarse de alguien	to fall in love
el amor	love
conocer a	to meet
se conocen	they meet / know each other
el novio / la novia	boyfriend / girlfriend
estar casado	to be married
una pareja	a couple *(pair)*
juntos	together *(roads at junction)*
una cita	a date
un beso	a kiss
un abrazo	a hug
contar con	to rely on *(count on)*
estar divorciado /-a	to be divorced
estar separado /-a	to be separated
discutir	to argue
llorar	to cry
echar de menos	to miss
la echo de menos	I miss her
embarazada	pregnant

Adjectives to describe people
grande	big
pequeño /-a	small *(like a Pekinese dog)*
alto /-a	tall *(altitude)*
bajo /-a	short
delgado /-a	thin *(delicate)*
gordo /-a	fat
viejo /-a	old
joven	Young

Positive Adjectives
simpático /-a	nice
alegre	cheerful
hablador /-a	chatty
trabajador /-a	hardworking
interesante	interesting
divertido-a	fun *(diverting)*
gracioso/-a	funny *(gracias for being funny)*

valiente	brave *(valliant)*
fuerte	strong *(a fort is strong)*
cariñoso /-a	kind
amistoso /-a	friendly *(from amigo)*
guapo /-a	goodlooking
deportista	sporty

Negative Adjectives

antipático /-a	not nice
triste	sad
terco /-a	stubborn
aburrido /-a	boring
serio /-a	serious
débil	weak *(a debilitating illness)*
tacaño /-a	mean
travieso /-a	naughty
pesado /-a	annoying
feo /-a	ugly
perezoso /-a	lazy
orgulloso /-a	proud

Some lovely cognates (no translation necessary!)

activo /-a	imaginativo /-a
tímido /-a	impulsivo /-a
modesto /-a	intolerante
arrogante	optimista
ambicioso /-a	pesimista
artístico /-a	popular
agresivo /-a	religioso /-a
prudente	reservado /-a
creativo /-a	romántico /-a
convencional	sarcástico /-a
generoso /-a	superficial
desorganizado /-a	sociable
elegante	diplomático /-a
famoso /-a	tradicional
fascinante	inteligente
atlético /-a	estúpido -/a
contento /-a	
culpable	

Qualifying your adjectives
siempre	always
a veces	sometimes
a menudo	often
muy	very
bastante	quite
un poco	a bit
más / menos…. que yo	more / less … than me

Hair adjectives – tengo el pelo…
largo / corto	long / short
liso / rizado	straight / curly
rubio / marrón	blonde / brown

General appearance
lleva gafas	he wears glasses
una barba	a beard *(like barbed wire)*
bigote	moustache *('e got a bigote)*
parezco a mi madre	I look like my mother
nos parecemos	we look like each other

Example
Mi hija tiene el pelo rubio y largo y los ojos marrones. Es muy inteligente, pero a veces un poco tímida, y menos extravertida que yo. Normalmente nos llevamos bien porque tenemos muchas cosas en común como el deporte, pero a veces discutimos cuando sale con sus amigas en vez de hacer sus deberes.

My daughter has long blonde hair and brown eyes. She is very intelligent but sometimes a bit shy, and less outgoing than I am. Normally we get on well because we have a lot in common like sport, but sometimes we argue when she goes out with her friends instead of doing her homework.

Clothes and things you carry
una camisa	a shirt *(camisole)*
una camiseta	a tshirt *(litte camisa)*
pantalones	trousers *(pants are long)*
vaqueros	jeans
un vestido	a dress *(long vest)*

una falda	a skirt *(folded pleats?)*
una chaqueta	a jacket
un jersey	a jumper
un abrigo	an overcoat
un impermeable	a raincoat *(impermeable)*
calcetines	socks *(concertina down legs)*
zapatos	shoes
zapatillas de deporte	trainers
los guantes	gloves
un cinturón	a belt *(from cintura=waist)*
una corbata	tie *(bat things away with it)*
un gorro	woolly hat
gafas	glasses
un paraguas	umbrella *(para agua = for water)*
un monedero	wallet *(your money der)*
una maleta	suitcase *(need a mallet to shut it)*
una bolsa	a bag
un reloj	a watch or clock

Describing clothes

rayado /-a	striped
a cuadros	checked *(quadrants)*
ajustado /-a	tight *(needs adjusting!)*
con puntitos	spotty *(punto = dot)*
de cuero	leather
de lana	woollen *(from a llama?)*
de seda	silk
de algodón	cotton *(coddon)*
la moda	fashion
la marca	the brand

Colours

rojo /-a	red
naranja	orange *(norange)*
amarillo /-a	yellow
azul	blue *(azure)*
marrón	brown
rosa	pink
gris	grey
blanco /-a	white

negro /-a	black
verde	green *(verdant)*
morado /-a	purple

HOUSE, HOME AND ROUTINE

una casa	a house
un piso / un apartamento	a flat
la planta baja	the ground floor
el primer / segundo piso	the first / second floor

Structure

el edificio	building *(Eddy fixed it)*
la ventana	window *(for ventilation)*
la puerta	door *(port is a door to a country)*
las paredes	walls *(a pair of Eddy's constructions)*
el tejado	roof
el techo	ceiling

Rooms

la habitación	room *(you inhabit it)*
el dormitorio	bedroom *(dormitory)*
la cocina	kitchen
el jardín	garden
el salón	lounge *(saloon)*
el garaje	garage
el vestíbulo	hall
el comedor	dining room *(from comer=to eat)*
el despacho	office *(send dispatches from here)*

Furniture etc

los muebles	furniture
el armario	wardrobe *(put arm in, get armour out)*
la cómoda	chest of drawers
la alfombra	rug
la cama	bed
la almohada	pillow
la estantería	bookshelf *('it stand here')*
el lavaplatos	dishwasher
la lavadora	washing machine

el grifo	tap *(grip it)*
el espejo	mirror *(looking 'especially' lovely)*
el horno	oven
el césped	lawn
el árbol	tree
la hierba	grass *(green herbs)*
las flores	flowers
detrás de	behind *(leave trash behind)*
delante de	in front of *(you leant on it)*
al lado de	next to *(a lad next to a lady)*
cerca de	near
compartir	to share *(into compartments)*
limpio	clean *(limp after all the cleaning)*
sucio	dirty
desordenado	untidy
los vecinos	neighbours *('they've seen us!')*

Household chores

pasar la aspiradora	to do the hoovering
poner la mesa	to lay the table
quitar la mesa	to clear the table
lavar los platos	to wash the dishes
preparar la comida	to do the cooking
arreglar mi dormitorio	to tidy my room
ayudar a mis padres	to help my parents
lavar el coche	to wash the car
limpiar la cocina	to clean the kitchen
hacer jardinería	to do the gardening
sacar la basura	to take out the rubbish *(in a sack)*
hacer de canguro	to do babysitting *(with baby in pouch)*
llenar el lavaplatos	to fill the dishwasher

TOWN AND TRANSPORT

la mejor región de…	the best region of
en mi barrio	in my area *(barriers protect)*
en la ciudad	in the city *(-dad ending = ity)*
en mi pueblo	in my village
mucho que hacer	a lot to do
vivo aquí desde hace	I have lived here for

ventajas	advantages
desventajas	disadvantages

Places in the town
hay	there is / are
un lugar	place *(lug your stuff there)*
donde se puede	where you can
un cine	cinema
restaurantes	restaurants
polideportivos	sports centres
colegios	schools
un centro comercial	a shopping centre
mercados	markets
supermercados	supermarkets
iglesias	churches
parques	parks
almacenes	department stores
tiendas	shops
la acera	the pavement
la zona peatonal	the pedestrian zone

Things to do in town
ver películas	to see films
comer	to eat
ir de compras	to go shopping
hacer deporte	to do sport
salir por la noche	to go out at night
pasear al perro	to walk the dog
dar paseos	to go for walks
descansar	to rest / relax
encontrarse con amigos	to meet up with friends
tomar una copa	to have a drink
estudiar	to study
seguir viviendo aquí	to carry on living here
aprovechar	to make the most of

Town negatives
lo que no me gusta	what I don't like
los atascos	traffic jams *(a task getting through)*
el tráfico	the traffic

la contaminación	the pollution
el ruido	the noise *(ruins it all)*
tirar basura	to drop litter
caro	expensive *(expensive car)*
la calle	the street
lleno	full

Shopping

ir de compras	to go shopping
abierto	open *(open 'a-beer-too'!)*
cerrado	closed *('there-are-no')*
dinero	money *(dinner money)*
el descuento	discount
hacer cola	to queue *(for coca cola)*
gastar	to spend *(on gas bill)*
malgastar	to waste *(bad spend)*
una tarjeta de crédito	a credit card
no puedo permitírmelo	I can't afford it

Countryside

mudarse	to move house
en el campo	in the countryside
hay menos ruido	there is less noise
tranquilo	quiet
vacio	empty *(vacant)*
espacios verdes	green spaces
aislado	isolated

El transporte público

	public transport
en autobús	by bus
en tren	by train
en coche	by car
en barco	by boat
en bici	by bike
en avión	by plane *(aviation)*
a pie	on foot
voy andando	I walk
caro	expensive *(expensive car)*
barato	cheap *(cheap bar)*
la estación de trenes	the train station

la parada de autobuses	the bus stop
rutas para ciclistas	cycle paths
una red de transporte	a transport network
tardo una hora en ir al…	it takes me an hour to get to…

EDUCATION

el mejor colegio	the best school
la mejor universidad	the best university
del mundo	in the world
lo que más me gusta	what I like most
los profes	the teachers
los alumnos	the pupils
se comportan	they behave
mal / bien	badly / well

Facilities
aulas	classrooms *(teacher = wise owl)*
laboratorios	laboratories
una biblioteca	a library
un comedor	a dining room
campos deportivos	sports fields
una piscina	a pool
el patio	the playground
donde se puede	where you can
jugar	to play
charlar	to chat
estudiar	to study

Education verbs
enseñar	to teach *(you need to be 'senior')*
aprender	to learn *(an apprentice learns)*
sacar buenas notas	to get good marks *(out of the sack)*
tener éxito	to succeed *(exciting!)*
revisar	revise
pasar exámenes	to take exams
aprobar un examen	to pass an exam *(probably?)*
sacarse un reprobado	to fail *(reprobate!)*
suspender	to fail
preguntar	to ask

contestar	to answer *(in a contest)*
poner pruebas	to give tests

School day
al llegar	on arriving
las clases empiezan	lessons begin
la hora de comer	the lunch hour
el descanso	break time
el recreo	break time

School opinions
lo que más me gusta	what I like most
lo que no me gusta	what I don't like
tenemos que	we have to
llevar un uniforme	wear a uniform
los profes nos dan	the teachers give us
demasiados deberes	too much homework
las reglas son estrictas	the rules are strict
no se puede	you can't
comer chicle	to chew gum
usar el móvil	to use a mobile
llevar joyas	to wear jewellery
llevar maquillaje	to wear make-up

Plans for the future
seguir estudiando	to carry on studying
para que pueda	so that I can
conseguir un buen trabajo	get a good job
ayudar a la gente	to help people
ganar mucho dinero	to earn a lot
viajar por todas partes	to travel everywhere
cambiar el mundo	to change the world

Jobs
un empleo / trabajo	job
contable	accountant
abogado /-a	lawyer
hombre de negocios	businessman
profesor /-a	teacher
científico /-a	scientist

peluquero /-a	hairdresser
periodista	journalist
enfermero /-a	nurse
marinero /-a	sailor
escultor /-a	sculptor
escritor/-a	writer
pescador /-a	fisherman
bombero /-a	fireman
panadero /-a	baker
matador /-a	bullfighter
ingeniero /-a	engineer
cantante	singer
ama de casa	housewife

LEISURE

el ocio	leisure
en mi tiempo libre	in my free time
hago	I do
juego	I play
me gusta hacer	I like doing
me gusta jugar	I like playing

Sports that take hacer

deporte	sport
natación	swimming
equitación	horseriding
windsurf	windsurfing
vela	sailing *(turn the v round for the sail)*
patinaje	skating *(pat the ice)*
gimnástico	gymnastics
ciclismo	cycling
piragüismo	canoeing
tiro con arco	archery
alpinismo	mountaineering
atletismo	athletics

Sports that take jugar

jugar al ajedrez	to play chess *(a head-race!)*
jugar al baloncesto	to play basketball

jugar al fútbol	to play football
jugar al hockey	to play hockey
jugar al cricket	to play cricket

Sports events

un partido de fútbol	a football match
el jugador	player
el / la futbolista	footballer
el / la tenista	tennis player
el / la ciclista	cyclist
el / la atleta	athlete
el / la campeón /-a	champion
los espectadores	spectators
el partido	match
el torneo	tournament
el balón	ball
el campeonato	championship
la carrera	race
en equipo	in a team
entrenarse	to train
recibir premios	to win prizes
asistir a	to attend

Other hobbies

periódicos	newspapers *(about a period in history)*
libros	books *(library but libra = a pound £)*
leer	to read
revistas	magazines *(reveiws)*
novelas	novels
tebeos	comics
la lectura	reading
dibujar	to draw
pintar	to paint
dar paseos	to go for walks
ir de compras	to go shopping
escuchar música	to listen to music
ver la tele	to watch TV
tocar el piano	to play piano *(toc toc toc)*
cantar	to sing *(chant)*
bailar	to dance *(ballet)*

coleccionar	to collect
pescar	to fish

Cinema and TV

ir al cine	to go to the cinema
ver la tele	to watch TV
acabo de ver	I have just seen
trata de	it's about
una película	a film *(about pelicans?)*
mi pelicula favorita	my favourite film
mi programa favorito	my favourite programme
telenovelas	soaps
telebasura	rubbish TV
documentales	documentaries
las noticias	the news *(notices)*
educativa	educational
una herramienta	a tool *(hairy-men tools)*
una película de horror	horror film
una película de guerra	war film
una película policiaca	detective film
una película del oeste	western
una película de amor	romantic film
una película de aventuras	adventure film
dibujos animados	cartoons
efectos especiales	special effects
el canal	channel

Holidays

ir de vacaciones	to go on holiday
reservar	reserve
una habitación	a room
fui a …. con ….	I went to…. with…..
pasar	to spend (time)
había	there were / there was
el vuelo	the flight
el viaje	the journey *(voyage)*
un billete de ida y vuelta	a return ticket
al extranjero	abroad *(strangers)*
durar	to last *(endure it while it lasts)*
he perdido mi pasaporte	I lost my passport

he perdido el avión	I missed the train *(lost it)*
el retraso	the delay
hacer las maletas	to pack the suitcases
el equipaje	the luggage
seguro /-a	sure
la seguridad	security *(-dad ending = ity)*
alojarse	to stay *(lodge yourself)*
el alojamiento	accommodation
un apartamento	a flat
un albergue	a hostel
un camping	a campsite
el hotel estaba	the hotel was situated
cerca de la playa	near the beach
la arena	the sand *(from sandy arenas)*
la entrada	entrance
la salida	exit / departure
los servicios / aseos	toilets
la vista	view
llegar	to arrive *(on your legs)*
sacar fotos	to take photos
probar	to try
los platos típicos	the local food
tomar el sol	to sunbathe
mandar cartas postales	to send postcards
comprar recuerdos	to buy souvenirs *(to record visit)*
relajarse / descansar	to relax
divertirse	to have fun
conocer a gente nueva	to meet new people
salir a bailar	to go out dancing
me lo pasé bomba	I had a great time
tengo ganas de	I would like to
volver	go back
en el futuro	in the future
esperar	to hope / wait for

WEATHER

hace sol	it's sunny
hace calor	it's hot
hace frio	it's cold
hace viento	it's windy

llueve	it's raining
hay tormentas	it is stormy
hay niebla	it's foggy
nieva	it's snowing
la lluvia	rain
las nubes	clouds

Festivals

las fiestas	festivals
el Año Nuevo	New Year
la Navidad	Christmas
el árbol de Navidad	Christmas tree
la boda	wedding
el nacimiento	birth
la Nochebuena	Christmas Eve
la Nochevieja	New Year's Eve
la Pascua	Easter
mandar	to send
postales de Navidad	Christmas cards
encender velas	to light candles
un desfile	a procession
dar / recibir	to give / receive
regalos	presents

HEALTH, BODY, ILLNESS, ACCIDENTS, FOOD

Health

la salud	health
malo / bueno para la salud	bad / good for you
sano / saludable	healthy
unos consejos	some advice
llevar una vida sana	to lead a healthy life
una dieta sana	a healthy diet
una dieta equilibrada	a balanced diet
la cantidad	quantity *(dad= ity)*
cinco porciones de	5 portions of
fruta y verduras	fruit and vegetables
deberíamos	we should
intentar	to try to
comer sano	eat healthily

evitar	avoid
la comida basura	junk food
el azúcar	sugar
la materia grasa	fat *(greasy)*
el alcohol	alcohol
tomar drogas	to take drugs
fumar	to smoke
hacer ejercicio	to do exercise
hacer deporte	to do sport
al aire libre	in the fresh air
dormir	to sleep
puede causar	it can cause
enfermedades graves	serious illnesses
el cáncer	cancer
la obesidad	obesity
se puede	you can
enfermarse	to get sick
engordar	to get fat
aunque sea malo	although it's bad
para la salud	for your health

Illness

hay el riesgo de	there is the risk of
una enfermedad	an illness
estar mal	to be unwell
sentirse	to feel
toser	to cough
el tos	cough
vomitar	to vomit
estar constipado	to have a cold
un resfriado	a cold
el sida	AIDS
el dolor	pain
una picadura	a bite / sting
la gripe	flu
ir al medico	to go to the doctor
pastillas	pills
medicina	medicine
medicamentos	medicine

Accidents

un accidente	an accident
tuvo un accidente	he had an accident
el incendio	a fire
apagar el incendio	to put out a fire
el humo	the smoke
la inundación	the flood
el peligro	the danger
un pinchazo	a puncture
tuve un pinchazo	I had a puncture
el testigo	the witness
el riesgo	the risk
sangre	blood
una multa	a fine
ayudar	to help
salvar	to save
gritar	to shout
chocar / pegar / golpear	to hit
atropellar	to run over
ocurir / suceder	to happen
ahogarse	to drown
el herido	the injured person
la herida	the injury

Body parts

el brazo	arm
la mano	hand *(the main thing you need)*
el dedo	finger *(goes dead if you sit on it)*
el pie	foot
la pierna	leg *(longer than el pie)*
la rodilla	knee
la espalda	back
la cara	face
la oreja / el oído	ear
la cabeza	head *(cabbage)*
la nariz	nose
el estómago	stomach
el pelo	hair
los labios	lips
el diente / la muela	tooth

la voz	voice
los ojos	eyes
los hombros	shoulders
	(hombres - men have big shoulders)
la boca	mouth
	(for your bocadillo = sandwich)

Food and drink

comer	to eat
desayunar	to have breakfast
desayuno tostadas	I have toast for breakfast
almorzar	to have lunch
el almuerzo	lunch
cenar	to have dinner
la cena	dinner
la merienda	tea
la cocina	cooking / the kitchen
cocinar	to cook
pedir	to ask for / order
probar	to try

General food

pan	bread
tostadas	toast
cereales	cereal
mantequilla	butter *(meant-to-kill-ya)*
mermelada	jam
bocadillos	sandwiches
arroz	rice

la carne	**meat**
el pollo	chicken
un bistec	a steak
la carne de vaca	beef (*meat of cow*)
el cerdo	pig / pork
el cordero	lamb
una chuleta	a chop
el jamón	ham
la ternera	veal
el pescado	fish

las verduras	**vegetables**
las judías verdes	green beans
el pimiento	pepper
los guisantes	peas
la ensalada	salad
los champiñones	mushrooms *(champions)*
la lechuga	lettuce
el tomate	tomato
las zanahorias	carrots *(bigger than-your-ears)*
las espinacas	spinach
el esparrago	asparagus
la coliflor	cauliflower
las patatas	potatoes
las patatas fritas	chips
el pepino	cucumber
las cebollas	onions *(they-boil-ya)*

las frutas	**fruit**
la naranja	orange
las uvas	grapes
la cereza	cherry
el limón	lemon
las manzanas	apples *(man has Adam's Apple)*
el plátano	banana *(curls around a plate)*
el melocotón	peach *(peach skin feels cottony)*
la pera	pear
la piña	pineapple
el albaricoque	apricot
el helado	ice cream
los caramelos	sweets
los pasteles	cakes

las bebidas	**drinks**
una cerveza	beer
la leche	milk
un té	tea
un café	coffee
un vino tinto	red wine
un vino blanco	white wine
el agua	water

el zumo	juice
el hielo	ice

En el restaurante — **in the restaurant**

los platos	plates
el tenedor	fork
la cuchara	spoon
el cuchillo	knife
el vaso	a glass
el camarero	waiter
la cuenta	the bill
la propina	the tip

TECHNOLOGY

la tecnología	technology
soy adicto	I'm addicted
no puedo prescindir de	I can't do without
el móvil	the mobile phone
el ordenador	the computer
enviar mensajes	to send messages
ponerse al día	to get up to date
navegar el internet	to surf the internet
descargar	to download
películas y música	films and music
chatear	to chat online
las redes sociales	social networks
una página web	a website
ponerse en contacto con	to get in touch with
buscar información	to look up information
la intimidación	bullying
desconocidos	strangers
problemas de vista	eyesight problems
pegado a la pantalla	glued to the screen
perder amigos	to lose friends
volverse solitario	to get lonely
volverse triste	to get depressed
volverse adicto	to get addicted
causar accidentes	to cause accidents

TIME PHRASES

son las dos y media	it's 2.30
son las ocho y cuarto	it's 8.15
son las tres menos cuarto	it's 2.45
es la una menos diez	it's 12.50
a las dos	at 2
hoy	today
ayer	yesterday
mañana	tomorrow
la semana pasada	last week
la semana que viene	next week
el año pasado	last year
el año que viene	next year
el fin de semana pasado	last weekend
el fin de semana que viene	next weekend
a veces	sometimes
a menudo	often
siempre	always
nunca	never
normalmente	normally
cuando sea mayor	when I'm older
cuando era joven	when I was young

Days
lunes	Monday
martes	Tuesday
miércoles	Wednesday
jueves	Thursday
viernes	Friday
sábado	Saturday
domingo	Sunday

Months
enero	January
febrero	February
marzo	March
abril	April
mayo	May
junio	June

julio	July
agosto	August
septiembre	September
octubre	October
noviembre	November
diciembre	December

Mi cumpleaños es el nueve de mayo.
My birthday is 9 May.

WORLD

Austria	Austria
Belgium	Bélgica
Denmark	Dinamarca
England	Inglaterra
France	Francia
Germany	Alemania
Great Britain	Gran Bretaña
Greece	Grecia
Holland	Holanda
Ireland	Irlanda
Italy	Italia
Netherlands	Paises bajos (m pl)
Russia	Rusia
Scotland	Escocia
Spain	España
Sweden	Suecia
Switzerland	Suiza
United Kingdom	Reino Unido
United States	Estados Unidos
Wales	País de Gales
Africa	África
Asia	Asia

Australia	Australia
Europe	Europa
North America	América del Norte
South America	América del Sur

Nationalities

American	americano/a
Austrian	austriáco /a
Belgian	belga
British	británico/a
Dutch	holandés/a
English	inglés/a
European	europeo/a
French	francés/a
German	alemán/a
Greek	griego/a
Irish	irlandés/a
Italian	italiano/a
Russian	ruso/a
Scottish	escocés/a
Spanish	español/a
Swedish	sueco/a
Swiss	suizo/a

USEFUL PHRASES AND IDIOMS

Positive opinions

vale la pena	it's worth it
me pone feliz	it makes me happy
me hace reir	it makes me laugh
tengo ganas de	I feel like
ir de vacaciones	to go on holiday
espero con ganas	I'm looking forward to
tengo suerte	I am lucky
lo que más me gusta es que	what I like most is
tengo buenas notas	I get good marks
me lo pasé bomba	I had a great time
no puedo prescindir de	I can't manage without
¡Qué bueno!	How brilliant!
el mejor país	the best country

Negative opinions

Lo que no me gusta es que	what I don't like is
Lo que más me preocupa es	what worries me most is
Estoy harto	I'm sick of it
¡Qué pesadilla!	What a nightmare
¡Qué horror!	How horrible!

Tengo expressions

Tengo suerte	I'm lucky
Tengo ganas de	I feel like
Tengo frio / calor	I'm cold / hot
Tengo que	I have to
Tengo hambre / sed	I'm hungry / thirsty
Tengo quince años	I'm 15
Tengo razón	I'm right
Tengo miedo	I am afraid
Tengo prisa	I'm in a hurry

Idiomatic Expressions

Estoy fastidiado	I'm not feeling well
Tengo el pie fastidiado	I've hurt my foot
¡Estoy machacado / agotado!	I'm exhausted!
He currado un montón	I've worked really hard
Voy a pegarme un madrugón	I'm going to get up early
madrugador	an early riser
Llueve a mares	it's pouring with rain
Cuesta un ojo de la cara	it costs an arm and a leg
Se me hace agua la boca	it makes my mouth water
Tiene un humor de perros	she is in a bad mood
Gastarse un riñón	to pay through the nose
Harina de otro costal	another thing entirely
Dormir como un tronco	to sleep like a log

Other publications by Lucy Martin also available on Amazon:

How to Ace your French oral

How to Ace your Spanish oral

How to Ace your German oral

French vocabulary for GCSE

Spanish vocabulary for GCSE

The Common Entrance French Handbook

Brush up your French – a revision guide for grown-ups

The Advanced French Handbook

Ten Magic tricks with French

If you have any comments or questions on any of the content of this book, please do get in touch via my website
www.lucymartintuition.co.uk

Printed in Great Britain
by Amazon